Vic Reeves

ME:MOIR
VOLUME ONE

This paperback edition first published in Great Britain in 2007 by
Virgin Books Ltd
Thames Wharf Studios
Rainville Road
London
W6 9HA

First published in hardback in Great Britain in 2006 by Virgin Books Ltd

A catalogue record for this book is available from the British Library.

ISBN 978 0 7535 1225 8

The paper used in this book is a natural, recyclable product made from wood grown in sustainable
forests. The manufacturing process conforms to the regulations of the country of origin.

Designed and typeset by Virgin Books Ltd

Printed and bound in Great Britain by Mackays

Vic Reeves

ME:MOIR
VOLUME ONE

(with cover and illustrations by the author's own hand)

ACKNOWLEDGMENTS

With thanks to Ben Thompson for editorial supervision, Rod Willcox for the title, Chiggy and Jo at PBJ for managerial guidance, the two Stuarts, Natalie, KT and everyone at Virgin for all their hard work, and Mum for two introductions: one at the front of this book, and the other to life itself.

INTRODUCTION

It's funny to have a son who everyone else knows by a different name. He's always been Rod to us – or 'Roddy' when he was younger. I can't get used to people knowing him as Jim (which is what his wife calls him), let alone Vic.

I remember when the Beatles came out. He thought they were wonderful, even though he was only four at the time (I didn't really like them, as I was still into Glenn Miller and things like that). When he was a few years older, we let him decorate his own bedroom and he did this huge picture of Rod Stewart on the wall. We were never sure if the reason he liked him so much was because they had the same name, but it took us three whole pots of emulsion to paint over it after he'd left home.

Our Rod was always good at art. He used to win competitions. Once, he sent in a picture of Marc Bolan from T-Rex and won a prize from his sister's *Jackie*, but he didn't want anyone to know that he'd painted it because *Jackie* was a girls' magazine.

As a teenager, Rod always used to put his head round the door and shout, 'I'm going out now, Mum.' I'd ask him where he was going and what time he'd be back, and he'd just say, 'On the last bus.' Now he's written this book, I'm looking forward to finding out exactly what my Roddy was up to.

Mrs Audrey Moir
Darlington
January 2006

CHAPTER ONE

'I ballooned to a frightening ten stone by the age of three months...'

By all accounts, I was ejected from the warmth and safety of Mum's womanhood at 11.55pm, just short of my due time. Had I been expelled five minutes later I would have been born on 25 January – the same day as my father and grand-father.

I have always told people that I have the same birthday as my dad and grampy – a little white lie that makes a good story and injures no one, a maxim I have always employed and to good measure. But the truth is that I was born James Roderick Moir, in St Jimmy's Hospital, Leeds, on 24 January 1959.

I was eight pounds when I was born, healthy and of good cheer, yet the midwife suggested that it might be a good idea for Mum to feed me on Complan, the weight-gaining food supplement. This she did, and I ballooned to a frightening ten stone by the age of three months.

I became so corpulent so quickly that my mother was unable to pluck me from my cot and I was eventually prised out with an oar. To remedy the situation, a skip was later rented to accommodate my ever-increasing mass.

I presume that the midwife's medical advice was commonplace in the late 1950s, and was offered up to all new mothers. Indeed, scientific records confirm that the Earth's axis shifted an amazing twelve inches under the strain of a Britain weighed down with millions of colossal babies.

The reason for this bizarre dietary regimen is still a mystery, but it led to constant mockery when Mum wheeled me around in my reinforced haycart. Sanctuary was eventually found in weekly workouts at the local baby-gym, where young mothers could meet with their gargantuan progeny and watch them roll around for a couple of hours – floundering like sick elephants on crash-mats – before expelling what must have been tons of Complan-based dung into nappies made from army surplus parachutes.

Not before time, the government came to the rescue and banned the infant Complan diet before the UK could sink into the briny deep. It was replaced by a regime of boiled sprouts and dried egg, mashed into a glutinous soup and administered with wooden spoons. The baby weight problem quickly vanished, but was soon replaced by a fresh hell in the form of deadly gases permeating the land, and heavy taxes were levied to pay for smog patrols to dispel the noxious fumes.

*

As a child, I was known as Rod. This was because all the men in our family were first-named James. My grandfather was James Gatherer Smith Moir and he took the Jim moniker, being first in line. My dad was James Neill Moir, and he was known as Neill. This led to all manner of confusion with official letters and the like, especially when I began school and had to explain to the teachers why I wanted to be called a name other than the one clearly printed on the register. I eventually gave in and became Jim when I began work, but that was still a long time off.

James Neill Moir was a Linotype operator at the *Yorkshire Post*. His father and his father's father were also printers, and as far back as can be traced in the east coast of Scotland – where my dad's side sprang from – the Moirs were all involved in the paper industry.

He was a good man in every sense of the word. He worked hard and saved up enough money to have his own bungalow built in the up-and-coming Adel area of Leeds. Prior to that, he and my mum had lived in a grotty one-bedroom flat next to a grave-yard in Primley Park Road, the sound of screech owls keeping them awake at night. But they had a strong love for each other, and shared aspirations for a life improved.

I was installed into 20, New Adel Gardens and the cot which Dad had made in the garage – he made the cot in the garage, I wasn't living in the garage – was painted white and embossed with a pale-blue, moulded lamb, which I immediately took umbrage to, screaming for mercy.

I took umbrage equally at the sight of my father. As he rose over me and coochy-cooed at his freshly born son I was alarmed by the hairy protuberance on his face. Just what was that monstrous object hovering above his upper lip? And as if the moustache wasn't bad enough, his spectacles filled me with even greater dread.

I panicked and unleashed a banshee cry that awoke and unnerved not only the city of Leeds and all Yorkshire, but parts of Lancashire as well. Clutching pitchforks, cudgels, and whatever else they could lay their hands on at such short notice, the neighbours flocked to the scene of the unearthly baying and burst into the house, valiantly prepared to defend their community from the horrifying brute that had penetrated their domestic enclave.

Their anxieties were allayed when my mum gestured towards the cot, where her newborn son was in the throes of a bout of frenzied caterwauling. It was simply an understandable reaction to the sight of his father, she explained tactfully. Their worries overcome, they offered mingled congratulations and condolences, and trudged back through the snow to their quiet homes, still marginally worried as to what unearthly fiend had taken residence in their Yorkshire idyll.

In the days that followed, I grew to understand Dad's whiskers and specs, and in further weeks actually came to love them. The incident was not, however, my only brush with fear. In fact, my earliest memory is one of sheer unqualified terror – one that, once again, led to a bout of uncontrollable wailing.

Where we lived there was a ginnel, which to you heathens who are not from the North is a thin passageway between buildings. Anyway, this particular ginnel led from the end of our cul-de-sac to the shops on the main road. Mum pushed me there in my colossal pram, the type that can only be described as a Thames barge with cartwheels attached, beneath a hood the size of a bus shelter. Propelling this titanic brute must have taken a gargantuan effort on the part of my mother. She being a mere five foot one inch tall, a gust of wind regularly sent her into orbit and she was often captured on radar by air traffic control at Yeadon airport.

On the day currently under consideration, we somehow arrived at the shops without taking to the air, and she parked me outside a shop and went in to buy groceries, a practice which would rarely be undertaken nowadays, but then was common-place. (I doubt if the mammoth trolley would have fitted through the door anyway.)

At that moment, I recall looking up out of my pram and seeing a corrugated fence to my right. This alarmed me to the point of inducing another shrieking fit. What I thought it was I don't know – or maybe it was simply that Mum had left me alone – but my protestations certainly did the trick. She was back at my side in record time. And, even though I was probably only a couple of months old when the corrugated fence incident took place, I can remember it like it was yesterday.

*

When I was one year old, Mum left Dad in charge of me while she went off shopping. It was the first time my dad had been allowed to look after me, and he was brimming with confidence – a confidence that would be shattered by the end of the day.

It was a beautiful morning and we played in the garden – me on my new horse-headed tricycle, my dad prompting me to turn in circles until he eventually corralled me into the delphiniums. What fun we had. However, tired by our exertions, it was soon time to go back indoors for some lunch. On the way back in I decided – just for fun – to trip and slam my face into the back-door step, busting my lip in the most dramatic style. There was blood everywhere.

Dad quickly swept me up and ran a bath to wash away the gore so he could inspect the damage more clearly. I was plunged into the water and he began to gently mop my bloodstained mug. This

I took great offence to and in protest decided it would be a good idea to nut the taps using both my forehead and my eyebrows. It was beginning to look like a bloody massacre – the bath became a scarlet trough, and my tattered face now resembled that of Charles Laughton in *The Hunchback of Notre Dame*. I still have the scars.

By the time Mum returned, I had been thoroughly cleansed and sterilised, swathed in lint and plasters, and all my wounds had been dressed with various strips of material. I looked like an American quilt. Of course, it wasn't my dad's fault, and Mum understood that, but for me it was the beginning of a life of falling over things – and out of things, and off things. In fact, if I could go out of my way to stumble, plummet or collide with anything, I would.

Once, when I was three years old, I was playing on a patch of waste ground when I began to taunt a small terrier who proceeded to attack me, biting me on the hand. (Again, I still have the scars.)

Another time, I was playing at my friend John Baker's house, when he amusingly decided to lock me in his toy trunk until I begged for mercy and was released. When I got out, he hurled a piece of broken glass at me which cut my hand. (Yet again, I still have the scars.)

Perhaps these not-so-tragic events have been a catalyst, but timidity – in varying degrees – has followed me throughout my years. Even now, I spring out of my chair if a squirrel leaps onto my face whilst I'm watching the television. I react in much the same spineless way if a kraken rises from the depths, attacks my vessel and hurls me into the maelstrom.

Over the years, I have managed to control and quell this anxiety and transform it into a puffed-up boldness, combined with a psychological mindset that renders any brittleness invisible. If you are of a similar disposition you might like to try the following methods yourself.

For instance, should you have a worrisome work colleague who regularly attacks you out of the blue with a mallet, stand your ground and stare at him/her with crossed eyes and hum a single low note, thus giving them the impression that you are rather other-worldly and mysterious, and should therefore be given a wide berth.

I have employed this method on numerous occasions with almost total success. The only time it failed was at the age of twenty, when I was attacked by a cockney barrow boy for the crime of being from the North, and was roundly thrashed whilst I stood humming at him with bug-eyes. Happily, that traumatic event falls just outside this book's chronological remit.

Other survival methods I can vouch for include 'The Twist', where a dance is used as a distraction to foil your opponent. Any dance will do, but a casual, informal and not too vigorous one will probably work best. This technique can also be used to break the ice and make friends in tricky social situations, perhaps at a supermarket checkout, or clay-pigeon shoot.

While other children who were being bullied at school would cower up against the walls, pathetically uttering things like, 'Not the face,' 'My dad's a policeman,' or, 'Do you want money?' with one leg partially raised – presumably an involuntary movement to guard the genitals, and so secure the survival of future timorous weaklings – I could be seen stood in the middle of the playing field, gently swaying to a nonexistent beat, cock-eyed and droning, while bullies walked away from me, shaking their heads in confused despair.

These and similar techniques can be useful when confronted with aggressive humans, but an animal attack demands a very different approach. If I were, God forbid, to come face to face with a puma with an irritable skin condition like psoriasis or herpes, which had left the brute in a less than sympathetic mood, my initial reaction would be to run and climb the nearest spruce and wait for a helicopter to whisk me away with its rescue harness, allowing me the opportunity to urinate upon the big cat, safe in the knowledge that the beast was flightless.

This method is, however, quite useless if one finds oneself cornered. In such a situation, a more rugged and macho man would undoubtedly wrestle the savage brute to the ground, slit its throat with his bowie knife and, with assorted grunts and snarls, devour it raw. I, on the other hand, in my theoretical/psychological way, would be more inclined to hypnotise the animal with a series of slow and gentle hand movements, accompanied by steadily spiralling eyes.

With a single graceful motion, I would genuflect before it and present a handful of salve made from leaves and berries from the forest. The creature would sniff at the concoction and then look at me and tip its head to one side, the way that Steven Spielberg's puppets tend to do, with a look of benign confusion. I would apply the lotion to its diseased areas, the puma would sigh with relief, offer a thankful smile and then drift off into a peaceful sleep, allowing me the opportunity to run like the wind to the safety of the spruce. Anyway, that's probably enough survival techniques to be going on with for the moment. It would be a shame to lose track of our story at this delicate early stage.

*

On 11 October 1962, Mum presented me with a sibling, Lois Elizabeth Moir. She took after my father, with dark hair and brown eyes, while I – with fair hair and blue eyes – resembled my mother. The other principal difference was that I was born in St Jimmy's, while Lois was delivered in the coal shed.

There was a mighty gale blowing that night, and Mum had gone outside to collect some fuel. She hauled open the door of the coal shed and entered, stooping to gather the tinder. At that moment, an especially potent gust raged through the garden, slamming the door shut and knocking her onto the sooty pile.

A bloodcurdling cry rang out from within the coal chamber, alerting Dad, who was indoors at his repast. He rose from his plate, a look of confused apprehension on his face and a pork sausage dangling from his mouth. He looked like Winston Churchill with piles.

Hurling his chair across the room – narrowly missing a visiting chaplain – he sped into the garden to find the source of the cry. Throwing the shed door open, he was confronted by the disturbing image of my mother's supine form blackened from thrashing about on the coals.

'What is the meaning of this outburst?' he bellowed imperiously, the sausage still in its earlier position. 'I was dining in the presence of a visiting chaplain, when I heard a distant cry – one of anguish, even despair – and now I discover it is you, my wife, languishing upon the coal pile. Offer me an understanding of this confused scene, woman.'

'I am in the throes of childbirth, husband. I fear the child comes. Make preparations instantly, there is no time to spare. Fetch hot water, lay down your cloak here on the damp coals, and prepare to deliver the infant forthwith, as I am in great and plain anxiety.'

Father drew the waters and laid down his cloak, and the child was born: a beautiful black-haired girl. Safely delivered in the dark shelter, she was named right there upon the coals: Lois, after our Alaskan aunt, and Elizabeth, after our good queen Bess.

Of course my parents didn't really speak in this absurd, Miltonesque way and my sister wasn't born in a coal shed, but that is the way I choose to imagine the scene, so let that be the end of it.

(She was born at home though … in the larder.)

CHAPTER TWO

'The wallpaper was a kind of vomit-inducing vortex, presumably designed using diagrams of the giant maelstrom off the coast of Norway'

My mother's mother was Lillian Leigh. She was married to Simeon Leigh who had died in 1949, being 30 years older than Lillian. It was later revealed that he had married before, had three sons, and abandoned them all, before bigamously marrying my grandmother.

Their early life – and that of my mum – had been spent either moving around from village to village as my grandfather went in search of various dead-end jobs or signed on the dole. This was odd, as he came from a well-to-do family of butlers, and was always impeccably dressed in fine suits and spats with a fresh flower in his lapel. But when Simeon died, after belated complications due to the injuries he had received when buried in a First World War trench, Grandma moved to Moortown in Leeds, a couple of miles from Adel.

She lived there with my Aunty Ada – a woman of frightening appearance, black and grey hair cut into a short back and sides, thick horn-rimmed glasses, and military-style garments. Ada's views were in line with her stern demeanour, and she believed that children should be regularly beaten with birches and cat-o'-nine-tails.

My sister and I would cower when she entered the room and hide in the scullery until we were sure the coast was clear.

She was the antithesis of our grandma, who was the sweetest woman in Yorkshire (and, by the way, Ada wasn't our real aunty, but Grandma's friend and companion).

I remember one memorable argument between Aunty Ada and my mum while we were out walking one summer's evening. Ada had begun by insisting that Harry Secombe was the greatest singer ever and Mum had disagreed. This trivial difference of opinion escalated from a mild difference of opinion, to bickering, to all-out civil war – much to my amusement. The walk continued in silence with Aunty Ada looking daggers at me as I stifled my giggles.

In order to get to Grandma's house, we would load up the giant pram with provisions and head off into the woods, rattling over roots and branches in the general direction of Moortown.

I would, of course, attempt to climb onto the pram that now housed Lois, along with the provisions, much to the annoyance of Dad, whose job it was to shove it through the forest while being constantly berated.

About halfway through the woods, there was a river. When we reached this point, Dad would bundle us all into the monumental pram, take out his ever-present paddle, launch us into the flow and row us across to the other side where we all disembarked and climbed the steep bank before us.

Once at the top of this ridge we were confronted by a long,

wide metal pipe that crossed a small ravine. We were ushered into this pipe and hurtled through it, before being jettisoned at the other end into Grandma's street. I always loved these trips through the woods, and we were rewarded at the other end by Grandma's beaming smile and a bottle of Tizer (not to mention a lovely scowl from Aunty Ada).

*

For trips further afield, Dad drove our family around in a Bond Minicar; a tiny, three-wheeled chariot, powered by a 125cc Villiers motorcycle engine, with the four of us wedged into it like sardines.

Prior to this, and before we were born, Dad rode motorcycles, Nortons in particular. He and his friend Peter Scott often went to the TT races on the Isle of Man, as well as entering their own road races. And this love of bikes was echoed later by myself, as they were my first form of motorised transport, especially '50s and '60s British bikes like the ones my dad had ridden. Anyway, the next step for a motorcyclist planning to move into covered transport was the three-wheeler, because you could drive them on a two-wheeler licence. Hence the Minicar.

Every weekend we would travel around the countryside, visiting castles, gardens and ascending hills and mountains from the North Yorkshire Moors to the Lake District. Trying to encourage the Minicar up one-in-four gradients and around snaking mountain passes proved an anus-clenching experience, the vehicle regularly veering wildly off the road into tarns or sliding backwards down scree slopes. In icy conditions we would desperately struggle up the hills, wheels spinning wildly and a look of grim determination on Dad's face as he willed the thing along.

One time, we were returning from a camping trip to Filey in diabolical fog (whenever we went camping, which was very often, it always seemed to be in adverse weather conditions). There was a pile-up on the road and we rammed into the back of a Commer van. Dad left us in the car and went off to seek assistance.

The dense fog swirled around us – a sickly, yellow pea-souper, enveloping us with its threatening gloom and penetrating the car with creeping nicotine fingers. Dad eventually returned with a tow truck, and we set off home in our crippled three-wheeler, our camping equipment, pushchairs and luggage still Sellotaped to the roof. And that was the end of the Bond Minicar.

Dad then turned to four-wheelers – especially Renaults – but also had a brief fling with a Moskovich, a car that should, by rights, have never been allowed out of the USSR. It was only driven by Politburo clerks and apprentice mafia youths, and resembled a shoebox filled with seats made from melted-down margarine tubs.

I think Dad selected this appalling automobile because of its fuel efficiency. By all accounts you could travel the length and breadth of Russia seventeen times without it drying up.

*

In 1964, aged five, I began primary school. The fire station – where I was initially tutored – was just a short walk from home. Huge great red sliding doors opened to the spacious interior which was used to house the fire engines, and off to the right was the small room with high windows that was our classroom.

Like most of the other children, I was petrified at leaving the homely warmth of what we had known in our tender years. Torn from our mothers' bosoms and the sanctum sanctorum of our respective bungalows, we were ripped from our fathers' fortitude and thrust into an unknown arena to be lorded over by a new governess alongside children we didn't know.

Who was this woman who had replaced our mothers and why should we surrender to her authority? We screamed and kicked and launched our lunch at the walls – banana sandwiches and teacakes stuck to every corner – as we were abandoned by our equally distraught parents. But being subservient infants, we soon gave way to our new mistress, and nervously settled into our new world.

'Good morning children. My name is Miss Wilson and I am your teacher.'

'You're not my mum,' screamed Hayley Dobson.

'I want my doggy,' yelped Brian Holthorpe.

'Bleeaaarrrggghhhhh!' offered John Reynolds.

I took a slightly different tack: 'Belay there, shipmates,' I pronounced forcefully, 'let's hear what our new captain has to say before we condemn her.' The noise quickly abated, calm descended and Miss Wilson once again addressed her crew.

'Thank you, Roddy. Now once again, I am Miss Wilson and the first thing we shall do today is try to write our names. Can we do that?'

'Yes, Miss,' we sang, and were issued with scraps of sugar paper and wax crayons to scrawl with.

Tongues out and hunchbacked, we set crayon to paper and began to make our marks, which were collected by Miss Wilson and scrutinised. We eagerly awaited the results as poor Miss Wilson attempted to decipher the hieroglyphics.

'Hands up, Joug Potklder.'

No one responded.

'Hands up, Hairy Begtdjxk.'

Silence.

'Ah, here's one ... Roderick Moir.'

Victory was mine, praise the Lord. Informal handwriting lessons held by Mum had earned me the prize of being the only child in the room able to declare themselves to be in a state of literacy. I was king of the class. I puffed out my chest, stuck my hands on my hips, and held my chin in the air. I paraded around the classroom like Mussolini, looking down my nose at my failed peers.

'I am the winner, I am the winner, you are all losers 'cos I am the winner,' I chanted cockily, until some whispered words and the guiding hand of Miss Wilson set me back in my chair.

On collection from my first day at school, I excitedly told Mum of my triumph, and was rewarded with an ice-pop and a packet of Parma Violets and later – when Dad returned home – a Dinky toy Austin 7. This seemed like it might work out all right. Tomorrow I would write my name again and receive more gifts.

Sadly, that wasn't the way it worked, as the next day we had to count and write numbers on our sugar paper. I was a dismal failure and my earlier pride was replaced by the dunce's cap reserved for the most simple-minded and vapid of children.

Whilst I enjoyed my time at the fire station – endlessly writing my name and waving it in front of Miss Wilson – it was to be short-lived. New technology meant that many jobs at the *Yorkshire Post* were in peril. And one of these was Dad's.

He had been offered another position at the *Northern Echo* as a Linotype operator – working nights, typing the news and racing results on a giant black typewriter. I once saw him operate this monster and his fingers sped across the keys like lightning – a skill I wish I had inherited, in view of how long it is taking me to type this book.

While I was at school – and unbeknownst to us – Dad had been on several exploratory trips to the area around Darlington where the *Northern Echo* was based, searching for a new home for us. Pretty villages like Hurworth and Barton were considered, but all proved too distant and/or expensive, and eventually one day he returned home with some news.

We were having tea when he made his announcement: 'Family, we will shortly be leaving this home, this city and indeed this county, and remove ourselves to a distant land beyond the boundaries of our beloved Yorkshire. We shall travel far to a new realm, a province known locally as "County Durham, the land of the prince bishops", the kingdom where Cuthbert found his final resting place. In short, pack your bags – we're off!'

A mixture of excitement and trepidation hung about the table like a pair of frillies dangling from a washing line. 'What news is this, Father?' I squealed. 'How can this be when we are prosperous and flourishing, our table is well laid, the house in good repair, and we are content?'

'Fear not, child,' Mum asserted. 'This land of which your father speaks holds great fortune for us. We shall valiantly tread this new soil with hearts of lions.' And with those sage-like words ringing in my head I retired to my bedroom and began to pack my worldly possessions – my Dinky toys and my teddy.

*

A few years ago, I returned to 20, New Adel Gardens and the home I hadn't seen for 35 years. As I approached, I felt an enormous sense of nostalgia, but also a measure of anxiety. Where had the time gone? I was halfway through my life, yet it seemed like just a few moments since this was my childhood home. I recognised everything and slipped into the kind of silent inertia that can only be induced when confronted with the distant past, in conjunction with an unknown future, and a sudden awareness that we only exist for a moment.

Cheery stuff, but I lightened up a little as I stood outside number 20. The house number sign my dad had made and painted was still there, screwed to the wall outside.

The people who lived there now were a lovely old couple – a lady and her father. He was a conductor in a symphony orchestra and had also climbed Everest. He slept in my former bedroom and the mementos of his life were crammed into the small space – photos of his time with the orchestra, his arrival at the summit of Everest, and his ice pick. I recalled lying awake in this very room every Friday night, waiting for my dad to return home with a Dinky toy.

In the sitting room, we had tea and macaroons while the lady of the house told me that after various enquiries the only information she could gather about my younger self was that I was a serial garden-piddler, regularly seen weeing in the neighbours' front gardens (a practice I'm glad to say I have since discontinued).

In the late 1950s and early '60s, our sitting room was decorated with a leopard-skin print carpet and a green and black leaf-print three-piece suite — very garish and faux organic — with an Ecko television in the corner that tendered both channels from its enormous ten-inch screen at selective times of the day. Postwar austerity had given way to swish opulence: a new kind of vivid iridescent vulgarity that everyone considered the norm.

As far as I can remember, the wallpaper was a kind of vomit-inducing vortex, presumably designed using diagrams of the giant maelstrom off the coast of Norway, where sailors are sucked to their doom in a monstrous whirlpool, and transferred to print by some young, avant-garde design student who'd never had any desire to actually live with this chaos.

Back in the present, number 20 had been transformed into a scene of placid modernity, the calm of current times replacing the fire of my infancy. The thing that really struck me was the height of the window ledge looking out onto the road. I remember looking out, hands on the sill at face height, waiting for Dad to return in his Bond Minicar from wherever he'd been, and now it was at groin level.

I said my goodbyes to the lovely couple and fled the parish, wondering if I'd return again in another 35 years — by which time I shall be either bathchair-bound, mentally infirm or have perished. Or perhaps I may still have enough juice in me to piddle in the garden and vanish, giggling up the ginnel.

CHAPTER THREE

'Join on for "Japs & Commandos", no girls allowed'

It was October 1964, and we were moving. Looking back through the rear window of the car, down the wide avenue that took us out and away from Leeds, I felt a great sense of loss. I gazed with an early twinge of nostalgia at the vanishing city – the place I had only known for five years, yet a place I had grown to love. I was unseated.

Our new home would be 59, Hewitson Road in Darlington – a 1950s semi-detached house on the outskirts of the town. When we arrived, the Pickfords removal lorry was waiting, filled with our furniture. The great thrill for me on entering was the fact that we had stairs, a novelty that I greatly abused – much to the annoyance of my parents and the removal men – by charging up and down them until my shoes were stripped of their soles.

My bedroom was at the front of the house and I settled in instantly, my Dinky toys carelessly thrust beneath the bed in their box, and my teddy delicately hurled onto the bed. We were installed. Yet more change was coming: the next day I would begin at my new school, Eastbourne Primary.

In my first five years in Adel Road, I had developed a strong Leeds accent, though I was, of course, oblivious to this. As I settled into my position in the classroom on my first day, I was asked by my new teacher Mrs Harris to declare myself, who I was, and what my intentions were.

'My neem is Raderick Mawyer,' I proclaimed, as guffaws erupted in the room, 'and I have just mooved 'ere frum Leeeds.' The hilarity it caused among my fellow students was rich and even Mrs Harris was on the floor in a foetal position desperately clutching her stomach in fits of laughter. Children were banging the tables and pulling out their hair, biting their satchels and ramming their rubbers into their mouths in order to staunch their hysterics. The headmaster Mr Cheeseman, who could not fail to hear the unrestrained cacophony of snorts, snickers and giggles, came to investigate.

'What is the meaning of this outburst?' he bellowed.

'Say it again, Roderick,' Mrs Harris managed to gurgle, through a veil of tears. I stood and once again made my bladder-rupturingly amusing claim to being of Yorkshire origin. Mr Cheeseman collapsed beside Mrs Harris and expelled a fart as he gasped for air. I had unwittingly presented my first gag. Thinking 'What the heck, if you can't beat 'em ...', I too burst into gales of laughter. I hoped this was the start of my acceptance into the school, and I think it was.

I quickly made friends at my new school, my best friend being Andrew Parlour, a boy with hair that resembled an ice cream; a thick bush of luxurious woolly blond curls that erupted from his crown to a height of approximately six inches. I was deeply jealous of this fleecy mop and would make informal requests to poke my finger deep into its pile, to mould and generally tease it into never-before-seen shapes – some beautiful, some terrifying.

Andrew lived in the next street, Lynton Gardens, in a house similar to ours. We played like any other boys in our five-year-old ways – sending our toy cars plummeting to their doom over kerb-stones and making specially formed ramps from Ricicle packets. On a daily basis, at least three hundred major accidents occurred at our omnipotent hands.

We were gods of destruction, but with a suitably supernatural power to revive both the passengers and the vehicles ready for the next day's destruction derby. Our toy cars could also fly, which meant that we could enjoy even more exciting crashes in the form of mid-air collisions. Sometimes I would gingerly suggest that I might be allowed to drive one of my cars through Andrew's hair, but this request was always denied.

Our after-school hours were spent down there in the gutter and on the kerb, orchestrating our disasters, until one day an older boy approached us. He was a slit-eyed lad of about nine, with hair that had been cut by a woodpecker and a face the shape and colour of a pancake.

'What you doin'?' he asked in a voice that demanded a response.

'Just playing,' we replied faintly, not looking up from our carnage.

'I'm playing too,' he proclaimed, and proceeded to produce an enormous ball-bearing. Lots of kids' dads worked at factories and foundries in the area, and therefore their fathers would bring home these giant steel balls as the ultimate marble, to be used to crush all opponents in a game of alleys. These ball-bearings were used in the manufacture of massive crankshafts for trains and earth-shifters and weighed about ten pounds. And this ball-bearing was the king of them all.

The pancake boy was well aware of the damage he could inflict on our puny tin cars, and all we could do was sit back and watch him crush them with his giant metal orb. We gazed on through eyes filled with tears as the ruthless fiend pounded and pulverised our world into submission – coupés, cabriolets, convertibles and concept-cars, all reduced to a formless pile of scrap.

'There,' he laughed, 'now there's a pile-up.' And he sped off, giggling, in the direction of the Firth Moor estate – his gait a lop-sided trot beneath the weight of his globe of destruction. We tenderly scooped up our devastated collection of twisted metal and vowed to destroy the pancake boy with fire, despite knowing that a trip to the Firth Moor estate was like a voyage into some terrifying jungle inhabited by wild and nameless creatures who would no doubt be hungry for our blood. Deciding against revenge, we abandoned our heroic plans and went indoors for a kind word of sympathy from Andrew's mum and some lemon barley water.

*

A few months later, I was once again round at Andrew Parlour's house. This time we were seated inside at a small table covered with a lace tablecloth and piled high with soda cakes, Battenbergs and fondant fancies, accompanied by the weakest of squashes.

We were seated in front of the Parlours' TV, the reason being that the event of the year – the funeral of Sir Winston Churchill – was being broadcast, and we had front-row seats. I recall this clearly, although I'm sure neither of us had the faintest idea who this bulky statesman was, and the solemnity of the occasion swept over us as we tucked into our tea.

The Parlours' front room had a kind of Edwardian sobriety – browns and creams battling with black-lined mahogany, only lightened by Andrew's glowing hair – much removed from the Moir household's bright, airy and modernistic design for living.

In our own sitting room we now had a black and gold-flecked suite offering not the slightest margin for comfort. This rested upon a mysterious green and gold Axminster, and the walls were a flavoursome burnt-orange woodchip. I loved it – it was home, and it felt that way.

I especially loved time spent in the kitchen – watching Mum toiling over the gas hob, preparing dinner. We were a healthy-eating family. Mum followed early guidelines for nutritionally correct foods, so we dined on new-fangled delicacies like green peppers and courgettes – commonplace now, but then it was the height of nouvelle cuisine.

Greens had an unfailing presence on our plates at dinner-time and I loathed them, the most abominable being – in order of least favouritism – green beans, Brussels sprouts, cabbage, leeks and, finally, peas. I found them vomit-inducing – literally: I only had to look at them and nausea took a grip. The smell brought on a sense of revulsion, followed by a biliousness comparable only to the sight of someone dining on dog nonsense, and when it came to actually eating this odious botany, I began to retch.

Dad would have none of it, and I was made to perch in front

of my plate until I had made vague headway into the vegetation. I jerked forward, puffing out my cheeks, making guttural sick noises and stifled belches as I stared at the plate, willing the toxic veg to vanish. Sadly, it remained in position, and I stayed there for what seemed like hours, until I mournfully raised a microscopic sample of cabbage to my mouth and, with eyes tightly shut, urged it in.

Once I had it in my mouth, as far as I was aware I had fulfilled my contract, so I declared that I had finished and asked could I please leave the table. Permission was not granted, and I sat there for another interminably long period until a cunning plan came to mind.

I would prove once and for all that this food was unfit for human consumption. I again raised my fork to my mouth bearing a barely visible fragment of leek, and after putting it in, I immediately fled the table and rushed to the lavatory to vomit – ergo, the food was pigswill. This still did not work. I was frogmarched back to the table, and the process began again.

'Third time lucky,' I thought, and whilst backs were turned I slipped as much greenery as I could into my trouser pockets. The remainder I carefully hid beneath my knife and fork, and repeated my plea, 'Finished ... may I leave the table?'

Mum and Dad carried out a cursory inspection of my plate. They looked at each other, nodded and replied, 'Yes, you see it wasn't so bad after all, was it?'

Yes, it bloody well was, I thought to myself. But I have foiled your plans to have me poisoned, and it is I who will have the last laugh.

I once again dashed to the toilet, thrust my hands into my pockets and unloaded my cargo into the pan. Even the touch of the revolting foliage brought me out in a sweat, but thankfully, and still heaving inwardly as I flushed the toilet, the vegetables disappeared. I returned to the bosom of the family happy in the knowledge that my secret was undiscovered, and with stealth and guile I could get away with it forever.

Inevitably, this was not to be. I became lax in my vegetable dumping excursions. A good soldier should always be vigilant – never presume that because you have completed several of the same missions without mishap, the enemy is not always watchful of your movements.

One day, I had blithely gone on one of my post-dinner-time sorties when I got waylaid by something or other and forgot to dump my load in the toilet. The following day, Mum was washing my trousers and, on turning out the pockets, amongst the bits of tissue, stones, sticks and rubber bands, discovered a veritable vegetable fusion. I was undone, my secret was out, and I was in trouble.

On returning home from school, I was presented with the evidence and forced to reveal my demented scheme to never eat veg again. Knowing that I was beaten, having no back-up plan and being too weary to concoct another, a compromise was reached. I promised to eat these green beasts only if they were offered to me raw. This was formally agreed upon, and from that day on, that's what I ate. Anything that was green was raw, and I grew to like it – raw broccoli, raw leeks, everything.

Nowadays I adore cooked vegetables – my favourite being cabbage smothered with butter. Yes, sir. But back then, my undiluted hatred of a steaming pile of greens consumed my every waking moment.

*

In our house, we had an Ecko television set, a ten-inch screen nestling within a gold-sprayed plastic and mahogany surround, with two dials for selecting your channel and then tuning in. 'The Goggle Box', as my dad called it, sat in the corner of the room and was used only occasionally and only for selective viewing. The furniture in our sitting room was arranged around the fireplace and not the television – the telly was an amusement to be considered when conversation had dried up or a monarch had perished.

But things began to change in the mid-1960s. Conversations in the workplace and in schoolyards started to revolve more and more around soap-opera characters and less around real lives. We were entering a new voyeuristic fictional age, and to maintain your place in society you had to be aware of Ena Sharples' port and lemon consumption or Ken Barlow's erratic love life. And so the television slowly began to take centre stage.

Armchairs were slowly eased round to face the screen, coffee tables were angled parallel to the tragic lantern ... but not in our house. The fireplace remained the family focal point and viewing was restricted to 'my programme', unless a formal written application was made requesting the viewing of a second programme which went before the committee – Mum and Dad – for clearance.

'My programme' was *Andy Pandy*. The sailor-suited and bonneted boy-puppet would emerge from his housing – a wooden toy-box – along with his mistress Looby Loo and assorted other living toys in order to plot the downfall of his master. Andy's master was a boy called Danny or Tommy or something like that, who seemed completely unaware that whilst he was absent his toy puppets would rise from their sanctums and gather round the prophet Andy and listen to his ramblings on life as a downtrodden marionette and how he could help them flee this penal institution.

I later graduated to become an avid viewer of *Supercar*, Gerry Anderson's super tale of a scientific family with a comical pet monkey named Mitch, and their adventures in the 'super' car they had invented. This was followed by *Fireball XL-5*, all about a space rocket piloted by heroic Steve Zodiac, and the magnificent *Stingray*, featuring the submarine masterfully skippered by Troy Tempest, his co-pilot 'Phones', and love interest Marina – a mute aquatic beauty who, in response to Troy's amorous approaches, looked astoundingly vacuous and ignorant.

Troy's arch enemy was Titan, the evil Neptunesque leader of a giant undersea nation of aqua-men, hell-bent on thwarting any land-dwellers' trips beneath the waves and into their realm. I loved this series, and would impress school-friends with impressions of the heroes, including comical scenes between smarmy Troy and the exaggeratedly vapid Marina, which were applauded by my peers because nobody liked her. She was a girl who simply got in the way of the macho men's undersea work.

I suspect Gerry Anderson was under pressure from his wife and puppet empire partner Sylvia to attempt to lure girls into this boy-dominated world. There could have been no other explanation for the truly laughable credit sequence featuring Troy singing a love ballad to a gormless-looking Marina, who appeared to have the DTs and wobbled uncontrollably throughout his crooning.

The same kind of principle applied to many of the films that I loved at the time. *One Million Years BC*, *When Dinosaurs Ruled the*

Earth and the *Sinbad* movies would all include a girl, scantily clad in a bearskin or a belly-dancer's costume, whose only purpose as far as I could see was to ruin any chance of the men destroying a giant turtle or locating the egg of the Roc by presenting the heroes with a heaving bosom, and thus distracting them from their task.

Of course, these women were featured not for the benefit of pre-pubescent boys like me, but for teenagers and young men to leer and ogle at. However any young man who could leer and ogle at Marina – a moronic, mute puppet – should have been instantly sectioned.

Mum and Dad's television restrictions were a sensible and family-orientated rule – designed to encourage conversation, game-playing and book-reading – from which I think I greatly benefited. On first leaving home, I took great delight in eating food in front of the TV, sitting very close to the screen and watching any old tripe that was on, but this rebellion was short-lived and didn't impress anyone.

*

Every few weekends, we would visit Dad's parents, Nanna and Grampy. I loved these trips. We would drive over the beautiful North Yorkshire moors to Seamer, near Scarborough, where they lived in a bungalow on a quiet road opposite a sheep field. As we arrived at their home and emerged from the car, the air was filled with the savoury scent of mince and onions. This – accompanied by mashed potato – was the staple meal on our visits as it was mine and Lois's favourite, and always seemed to herald the onset of a good weekend.

Nanna was a sweet and kindly old lady, with the whitest hair in the land and (to me) strange arthritic hands. She had an oddly pleasant smell about her – a mixture of marzipan and carbolic soap – and was also a terrific wit. Some years later, when she was near her end, she was living at my Aunty Rae's house. She spent her days sitting on her chair with a blanket over her knees and rarely saying anything.

One day, we were watching the news. Uganda's president Idi Amin was coming to Britain to visit the Queen. Nanna, after what must have been days of silence, piped up, 'Well, I hope he's brought his sandwiches with him.' I howled with laughter. Her comic timing was impeccable.

Grampy was gloriously eccentric, a powerful patriarch and devilishly funny. He was also a great educationalist. When we arrived at their home, I was always summoned to his study for an interview. He would make enquiries as to my progress at school, and then produce his ancient dictionary, a huge leather-bound lexicon that he had used when he was a boy. I was urged to open it at a random page and, eyes closed, blindly place my finger somewhere on the page, then open my eyes and see what word my finger had landed upon.

I was then asked to read the description out loud, and the next visit would have to use the previous visit's word in a sentence. I once uncovered the word 'conglomeration', and on my next visit was asked to use it in the context of what I had done that week.

'I went to school and there was a conglomeration of children there,' I declared proudly.

'Well done,' said Grampy, and I was rewarded with a look inside his heavily locked bureau – a cabinet I was constantly requesting entrance to.

The bureau was opened, and inside was nothing but various papers, scrolls, instruction manuals and tin boxes. I was disappointed, but desperate to locate some source of intrigue. A tin box caught my eye. It was beige, about five inches by two, and with three red blobs on it in a triangular formation. Beneath these blobs in gold lettering were the mysterious words *Dreipunkt – Cigaretten*.

'What does that say, Grampy?' I enquired.

'Three fingers,' he replied. 'You see, in the First World War, I was an infantryman, and every German I killed, I chopped his finger off and put it in this box.'

I was confounded, and further enquiries drew a blank. Not surprisingly, as during the First World War he was actually a messenger boy, cycling between the lines on a pushbike delivering orders – still an important and frightening job, but not the same as being an infantryman. And Grampy never killed nor chopped the fingers off anyone.

On prising open the tin I discovered his two war medals wrapped in toilet paper and the key to his Uncle Willie's fob watch. Years later I was given the box, and was now able to translate the words as 'three point – cigarettes', although I am still not entirely sure what the first part of this inscription means.

They were happy days at Nanna and Grampy's. We used to spend our summer holidays there – with our Aunty Rae and Uncle Norman, and our cousins Tim, Barbie and Pam – renting chalets on the front at Scarborough. The hours would pass quickly; I would spend them rolling around on the sand with my cousin Tim, writing bizarre poetry, playing dominoes with Grampy, and going

VIC REEVES ME:MOIR

to watch the model ship battles at dusk in Peasholme Park.

Grampy was always a bit of a small-time gambler, occasionally on the horses, but mainly the slot machines at Jimmy Corrigan's arcades. I would accompany him on these gambling excursions and he would impart such worldly wisdom as, 'Always drink your beer from a mug with a handle, otherwise you will turn into a woman,' 'Never leave the house without a monogrammed hand-kerchief,' and, 'Always keep a chamber pot beneath your bed,' (he had a gazunder beneath his bed at home, and I was offered a glance at its contents each morning).

We would return to the chalet after a trip to the arcade, coins jangling in our pockets, to be greeted with the happy scene of our united family.

Grampy was also incurably addicted to the adverts for new-fangled rubbish in the back of newspapers. He was forever sending off for electric boiled-egg slicers, or devices for turning the pages of a book without using your hands – pointless stuff, but he couldn't resist it. On one of our summer holidays at the chalet, he brought along a metal detector. The children were to take turns at sweeping the beach with his new toy, searching for coins that unlucky bathers had dropped, while he observed our progress from the roof of the chalet with a pair of World War Two binoculars, presumably removed from the hands of a U-boat captain just before he sank beneath the waves.

We would return each evening with our hoard and deposit it into a makeshift receptacle so it could be counted and stashed away. One day, Grampy came up with another money-making scam. This involved me wearing a sheet and a towel wrapped around my head. I was told to walk up and down the chalets, clutching a small tin bowl, and saying that I was a poor Arab boy in dire need of money for food.

This I duly did, and thoroughly enjoyed it, especially when I returned home with my pot brimming. And there was the same feeling of satisfaction when the holidays came to an end and we packed up and split off in our various directions – heavy with happy memories and thrupenny bits.

*

I was born less than fourteen years after the end of the Second World War, and Britain was still shaped by the lingering effects of the conflict. But by the 1960s, the immediate period of postwar austerity was giving way to a new explosion of free expression on the part of a generation of young people with no direct recollection of the hardships of wartime.

Shops like 'I Was Lord Kitchener's Valet' on the Portobello Road were selling second-hand military uniforms. Artists like Peter Blake and Richard Hamilton had introduced Pop Art into all corners of contemporary culture, and Britain was becoming fun again. People wanted to have a laugh, and I was one of them. For me, the impact of the war was diluted into comic strips and Airfix kits.

In the playground we would chant, 'Join on for Japs and Commandos, no girls allowed,' – although this seems to have been a game imported from America, along with its predecessor 'Cowboys and Indians'. We wore plastic Tommy helmets and played with Second World War tanks and aeroplanes and shouted out things like, 'Banzai' as we bombed into swimming pools. War comics were a staple diet for kids of my age, and swastikas and RAF roundels were drawn onto any available surface.

The swastika, or 'swazzi', as it was affectionately called, had a different meaning for us – it was as though after the war was won we had claimed it for mockery so it was no longer quite the evil, anti-Semitic symbol of dark destruction that it had been. In some ways, this was appropriate, as the Nazis had themselves stolen this mysterious symbol of life from Mycenae, Tibet, Greece, Africa and Lapland in order to turn it into a symbol of hatred.

German design was, on the whole, more stylish than the British, to my mind – from the suave uniforms Hitler allowed his henchmen to fashion for themselves, to the Heinkels and Focke Wulfs which looked more space-age and dynamic than our utilitarian aircraft (with the exception of the Spitfire). But the Germans lacked British spirit and we won the war, so balls to them.

I had a childhood obsession with those sky-bound embodiments of Nazi engineering prowess, and during play dogfights with our model planes I would always want to play the part of the ME109 or the FW190, and would quote dive speed and turning capability to my opponent as we fought aerial battles to the death.

My fascination was tempered one day when Dad discovered a secret hidey-hole I had in my bedroom – a floorboard that could be removed concealed a small collection of Nazi memorabilia: a Panzer tank (a model, not a real one), and a picture of Hitler I had cut out of a *World at War*-style magazine. 'What do you have a picture of this madman secreted beneath your floor for?' he enquired.

Of course, I had no idea whatsoever that 'millions of people died because of that man'. I felt ashamed and a traitor. It wasn't as if I supported Hitler in any way, so the hidey-hole was cleared out and the secret haul replaced with a cigarette case full of dried frogs and a picture of Boris Karloff.

CHAPTER FOUR

How undignified for I. action man to be tossed over wires

'I became the Sherpa Tensing of Darlington's outlying fields'

There was more to life at that time than Nazi dictators and dried frogs. I was making new friends in the area, and one of these was a boy who lived directly opposite us. Our meeting, however, was slightly out of the ordinary. I would look out of my bedroom window, onto the street, and occasionally be distracted by some curious and often baffling movements in the bedroom opposite.

It was a boy of about my own age, twisting and gyrating and striking highly unusual poses on his bed. Even more disturbing was the fact that he occasionally glanced in my direction; in fact, it often seemed as if he were doing it for my benefit.

Was it simply that he was practising his evening callisthenics, or was it some kind of primitive semaphore? I decided upon the latter and replied to his poses with equally queer stances of my own, ranging from the abstract, through Graeco-Roman attitudes and ultimately to the downright vulgar. These nightly exchanges became a regular occupation for us, and after a period we signalled that perhaps we should meet, presumably to discuss the merits of our unusual language of gesture. And so it was that we eventually came face to face, on neutral ground, in the middle of the street.

My new friend was indeed a strange boy, as I believe he must have thought me. His name was Peter Collins. He was the Titian-haired son of a farmer, whose luxuriant freckles suggested he had been following a muck-spreader for miles (maybe he had). We never discussed our semaphore sessions. Perhaps there was no need: it was just a naive and childlike way of making a connection. If this means of communication was practised by adults – say, for instance, my father to Peter's father – then not only eyebrows but also questions would be raised.

Peter Collins suggested that I might like to take a look in his dad's garage, as he had something there I might be interested in. I followed him into the dimly lit outbuilding. There was a faint smell of sawdust and rotting meat. 'Look, there,' he whispered, and perched on a shelf, filled with spanners and grips, was a large black crow, beady-eyed and staring right back at us. It was his pet.

'Wow!' I quietly squealed. 'Will it attack us?'

'Only if I give the command,' he replied, with enough authority to make me back away in the direction of the door. 'I've got eggs as well,' he announced, and showed me a shoebox filled with sawdust and small blown eggs – robin's, blackbird's, pheasant's and even a cuckoo's. This is, of course, illegal nowadays, but in the 1960s a lot of boys had egg collections in the bottom drawers of their bedroom chest, and I soon became one of them.

There were moral rules to our egg theft, in so much as we would only remove one egg from a nest and if there was only one egg then it must remain there. I became obsessive. Wherever I went I would be peering into hedgerows for nests, climbing trees and looking into hollows. I became an expert bird-watcher and observer of signs and evidence of their nesting sites. Eventually other boys would come to me for information and guidance. I became the Sherpa Tensing of Darlington's outlying fields, the Tonto of adjoining woodland, the chief egg man … but I never had a pet crow.

There was another kid up our street who had a bird. He was older than me and something of an enigma. He was a mod, and rode about on a scooter that he had chopped himself with extended forks – what would later become known as *Easy Rider*-style – and enough mirrors on the front of his bike to fill several Kentucky bordellos. As he sped by, eyes staring straight ahead behind coal-black shades, we cheered, not only because of his futuristic transport, but also because he had a kestrel perched upon his shoulder.

Rumour had it that he had a menagerie in his shed with all manner of birds, from eagles to the only remaining dodo; however, suggestions of a pterodactyl were dismissed as too fanciful. Nevertheless, this mystery man had trained his kestrel to roost at speed, and that could not be ignored. His gift for training his wild birds to do various acrobatic and impossible feats became legendary, and the fact that he never spoke a word raised him to a state of almost mythical celebrity.

This illustrious reign came to an abrupt halt one day, when the extended forks of his scooter gave way. He had made the scooter's modifications himself with his dad's welding kit, but clearly hadn't done a good enough job. As he tore by us, one fine June evening, there was a terrible crack and a snap and his scooter split in two, the front wheel and forks travelling onwards, the rear end screaming and whirring in the middle of the road – leaving him prostrate, bruised and weeping in front of it, the kestrel heading for Madagascar and freedom.

Neither he, nor his kestrel, was ever seen again, although years later Dad reported that he had seen him travelling down the Yarm Road at 2am in a souped-up invalid car, moving at speeds in excess of 90mph.

*

My consistent requests for a pet crow or kestrel were firmly rejected as rank folly, although there was an alternative proposed which necessitated a visit to my Aunty Elsie and Uncle Bert in Leeds.

Aunty Elsie had been a publican along with her first husband Jack. They ran the Globe public house in Meanwood Road. Sadly, Jack had a heart attack and died at Mum and Dad's wedding, and so Aunty Elsie sold up and moved to a small flat in Cardigan Road. Soon after, she met Bert – a short, jovial man, who was also widowed. They married, and became what appeared to me to be the happiest people in Leeds.

Their flat was an opulent Victorian affair with rich pub-style furnishings and a framed poster of a scene from *Swan Lake* above the fireplace. On entering their portals, Lois and I were always invited to delve into Aunty Elsie's handbag in order to retrieve some long-lost pre-war sweeties.

The opening of this bag would be accompanied by a flurry of sickly smelling powder. When the cloud had dissipated we could see inside all the wonders of the interior of the bag: compacts decorated with Quality Street ladies with parasols held aloft, faux gold lipsticks of varying shades of insipid pink, and handkerchiefs embroidered with hearts and forget-me-nots. From the depths of this grotto of wonder we would eventually lay our hands on an Everton Mint or a violet-flavoured lozenge, and repair to the sitting room to suck them.

The reason we were there on this occasion was to collect Joey, a budgie that had lived at the Globe with Elsie and Jack and had now outgrown its usefulness. Joey was a standard bird of its type – green and blue, prone to twittering, and eager to fly about the room on being released from its regular-sized cage. Nothing out of the ordinary with this feathered friend – even its name. After all, 99 per cent of budgies in Britain are named Joey. Joey definitely wasn't anything like as exciting as a kestrel, and even though it would perch on my shoulder, I doubted it would have raised my status in the cool ranks if I were to be spotted pelting down the street on my bike with a budgie in tow. I was nonetheless grateful and Joey joined our family, occupying a special position by the back window, being fed on cuttlefish bones and Trill bird food.

I loved to watch her (or him – we never did identify the bird's sex) flit about the room on missions to find the highest points available for landing. With her incessant chirruping and occasional packages of bird poo deposited without fail onto a crumpet or an occasional direct hit right in a cup of tea, she was the Bomber Harris of the bird world.

Joey lived with us for four years and became a much- loved friend. One day I was out shopping with Mum and had bought a plastic outline map of the British Isles. On returning home I proudly brandished the map in front of Dad, but there was a solemn atmosphere hanging about the home.

Dad sat us down and announced in a grave tone, 'I've got some distressing news: the bird Joey has perished. She fell from her perch at approximately 10.15am GMT and I have swaddled her in toilet paper in preparation for immediate burial.' I burst into tears and gazed at my plastic map, trying to come to terms with the bereavement.

It was the first time anything had died in my world – prior to that I hadn't considered mortality, I just presumed everything lived forever. Nevertheless I came to terms with the loss, and we buried Joey in the garden beneath a wooden gravestone with 'Joey' inscribed on it in biro. A few pertinent words were said, Dad being the orator, and we retired to the house for a solemn tea.

We were dealt another blow the following day, when Dad made a further announcement that Joey had been exhumed and devoured by next door's grave-robbing cat. I fumed and promised that I would have my revenge on this feline Burke and Hare. I never did, but soon after, to alleviate the trauma, Dad returned home with a replacement budgie – similar in every respect to our dearly departed Joey.

We installed the new bird into her cage and sat down to think of a name for it, eventually deciding – originally enough – on Joey. But was the new Joey as clever as the old Joey? Could she fly to the outer reaches of the sitting room and return to her cage without prompting? Could she accurately bomb our tea? It was time to find out. The cage door was opened and out she flew, twice round the room and out of the window. She had been in our company less than an hour and she was gone.

But the saga of Joey the Second didn't end there. Seven years later, Mum visited our neighbours – the Websters – and noticed that they had a budgie.

'We had one like that, some years ago,' she said.

'Oh, Joey,' replied Mrs Webster, 'she flew in through the window seven years ago to this very day.'

Yes, it was our Joey, the escapee. Mum immediately grabbed the startled bird and barricaded herself in our house, pursued by a confused and irate Webster family.

No, she didn't – she just returned home with the dramatic news and left it at that.

*

Pets were never really a feature in our house, although I did manage to persuade my parents to allow me a small catfish that I roguishly named 'Hitler', but, sadly, he didn't last long. Hitler was discovered floating upside down one morning – presumably after his bowl had been invaded by Russians and Americans during the night, and he had taken the cyanide tablet that he had secreted beneath his ceramic Davy Jones' locker.

I also kept a sand lizard that I flushed out from beneath a parked Ford Zodiac on my way home from school. I housed it in a shoe-box and cleverly named it 'Sandy', but soon after it died both of boredom and of the shame of being a sand lizard named Sandy.

I also reared mice in a cage in the garage, but I made the error of keeping a male and a female together and within seconds I had over 80 tiny white mice crammed into a small space. I did what anyone would do, and released them into the garden. After the pest control men had disappeared, it was announced that no more pets would be allowed on the premises.

There was one final dalliance with animal ownership though, in the form of a dog. After months of persistent badgering, I managed to persuade Mum and Dad to get a hound. One of Lois's friends' parents had an out of control mongrel that was prone to biting, yelping and laying turds on the carpet. It seemed like the obvious choice for a house pet – and it was free.

We collected the mutt from them one evening to the collective cheers of the neighbourhood and drove home beneath banners bearing the words 'Goodbye, devil hound' and 'Rot in hell, barguest!' We took the name of the animal with it, and Bengo was its name-oh.

I tried to convince my parents that it was a good dog, but the scars on my arms and legs where it had bitten me told another story. I would set my alarm and rise at 5.30am to scoop up its dirt and attempt to repair the furniture that it had spent the night gnawing, but my efforts were futile. Bengo was a menace and had to go.

Dad placed an advert in the paper saying 'Unruly dog for sale: a vicious, disobedient and uncontrollable canine fiend, would suit nobody, please relieve us of this evil creature, will pay.' Almost instantly, a raggle-taggle band of gypsies arrived on the doorstep and Bengo was loaded onto their cart to the applause of the neighbours. The enraged throng screamed abuse with pistols cocked, and bid the dog goodbye with cries of, 'Never again,' and, 'Boil it alive!' Bengo had gone, and never again would another pet gain admittance to our hallowed portals.

*

In the 1960s, Darlington was a stronghold for gypsies, and their encampments were visible all around the outskirts of town – as was their presence within the town itself. The sound of horse and cart clip-clopping along the streets was a regular event. Generally the cart was piloted by two gypsies on a mission to relieve people of household scrap, mangles that had ceased to mangle, rabbit hutches whose occupants had been murdered in the recent spate of rabbit killings we had been enduring, bicycles whose whistling owners had driven them into trees on their way back from a post-work gallon in the Wheatsheaf, and armchairs whose springs had sprung through the seats and begun to penetrate the buttocks of the sitter. These objects were gathered and taken to their camp-sites where they were piled up and left to mature for a couple of years.

The Hanrattys were the main hunter-gatherers and could be heard daily with cries of, 'Egg-bound! Egg-bound!' I asked Mum what 'egg-bound' meant and discovered that it was a term used to explain the difficulty experienced in delivering one's stools after dining on an excess of eggs.

It was true, there was usually a stool on the back of their cart, but what did eggs have to do with their delivery? I made further enquiries in search of an explanation: 'If you eat too many eggs, you get all bunged up and you can't do a poo,' came the reply.

'So why are the Hanrattys travelling around the neighbour-hood telling everyone that they're egg-bound?' I wondered.

Mum looked confused, 'What do you mean?'

'They go about shouting, "Egg-bound, Egg-bound",' I alerted her.

She thought for a moment. 'They are not shouting, "egg-bound",' she informed me, 'they are shouting, "Rag bone."'

Thank goodness for that. The thought of anyone coming to the assistance of somebody who was suffering from being egg-bound filled me with dread, and a series of unsavoury images appeared in my mind. Old ladies rushing out with brooms, bicycle pumps or vacuum cleaners, bending over and bidding the unfortunate Hanratty brothers to step down and bend over, or men clutching trowels quickly grabbed from their potting sheds.

Thankfully, these images soon vanished. 'Why do they shout "Rag bone" then?' I said. 'What on earth do they want with rags and bones?' Yet another ghastly image presented itself to me. This time it was a skeleton draped in the rags that its previously flesh-covered owner had perished in.

'Too many questions,' came the reply, as Mum hurled Joey's cage onto the cart, followed by a response from a Hanratty which sounded like, 'Dengue fever!' or perhaps, 'Ballast!' Mum turned and sped back into the house pursued by me and my further enquiries.

*

Another equine-powered visitor who made house-calls was Mr Todd, a travelling vegetable man whose covered wagon was laden with all manner of garden produce. Mr Todd was a sullen-faced individual who wore a trilby hat that was far too small for him. I can only presume that it was glued on to stop it from blowing off. He looked like a disappointed bloodhound wearing an organ grinder's monkey's hat, and his demeanour was one of getting his round done so as he could return home as soon as possible, sink into his armchair and die.

His arrival on the street was greeted by children gathering around and begging their mothers to buy carrots to feed Mr

Todd's horse, Eric. This was a great ploy by Mr Todd, as he never
had to pay for food for Eric. We paid for it, or at least our mothers
did. The horse was obviously well fed, as indicated by its incredible girth that dragged on the road as it gently and contentedly
sauntered along.

We would queue up and take turns at feeding the obese cob
until the women had got their supplies. Then Eric would produce
a rousing fart, present us with a mountain of steaming manure,
and trundle off to the next group of carrot-wielding kids. After
the cart was gone, men would appear with shovels and fight each
other over the prize-winning dung deposits laid along the street.

*

One of the other boys who would join me in feeding the
ravenous Eric was a big curly-haired lad called Stephen Hodgson,
or 'Hodgy', and he became my new best friend.

Hodgy lived at 22, Hewitson Road, and we would spend our
time together doing the usual things like trying to fish things out
of drains, attaching playing cards to the spokes of our bike wheels
so they sounded vaguely like motorbikes, and, of course, bird-
nesting.

Most people had a television, and those who did generally had
a black-and-white one, but Hodgy announced one day that his
mum and dad had got a colour TV. We went round to see this
marvel of modern times and were offered a demonstration. It
wasn't exactly what I was expecting. It was just their old black-
and-white telly with a piece of coloured transparent film ranging
from red at the top, through yellow in the middle and down to

blue at the bottom, Sellotaped onto the screen. The effect was, as you would expect, like watching a newsreader with red hair, a yellow face and wearing a blue shirt, or – if it was a western – a red sky with yellow horses galloping across what appeared to be the sea.

Still, you couldn't deny it was colour, and we watched it for hours until the television heated up and the cellophane buckled, distorting the images to the point that we were looking at primary-coloured newsreaders who appeared to have been plunged into a vat of acid, and westerns that had more in common with Timothy Leary than Sergio Leone. Eventually the Sellotape would melt, and the whole thing would peel off and lie down on the carpet in a steaming spectrum of limpid film, mercifully putting an end to our mesmerised state.

*

Hodgy and I developed an exciting pastime of trying to throw objects and get them caught on power lines in the hope of seeing them set alight or explode when a charge went through them.

Our favourite objects to ensnare on the cables were Action Men, and we would spend hours trying to get them to snag on the wires.

One day, Hodgy had a brilliant idea: 'We will go and find a stick and a bit of string and tie them onto the Action Man, that will make it easier to catch it over the wire. You go search in that direction and I'll look over there and if you find a stick or a piece of string, let out a shrill call.' That did it for me – 'let out a shrill call'. I fell down laughing: 'a shrill call'. I thought it was hilarious, and rolled around in fits on the floor for what seemed like days. When I eventually did stop howling, Hodgy was gone.

*

Our regular trips to visit Nanna and Grampy in Scarborough inevitably featured a visit to the Marine Gardens to listen to Max Jaffa and his band perform renditions of antique melodies to ancient people in deckchairs. The audience would be entirely hatted: the men wearing cream peaked caps and the women sporting ludicrously designed and coloured bonnets which were usually ball-shaped and featured various nets, floral devices and the occasional prong or stalk.

These preposterous head-coverings – often referred to as 'church hats' – were common among elderly ladies. And I recall Aunty Ada owning one particularly ridiculous lime-green affair with lily-shaped attachments, a tiny veil, and what appeared to be two aerials with grapes on the end of them, giving her the appearance of 'My Favourite Martian' after emerging from a stagnant swamp.

Sunday morning worship saw pews filled with a sea of these multi-coloured monstrosities – stems and shoots, nameless fruits, net curtains covering a purple globe or an orange bell-shaped bucket, the occasional butterfly or moth, and sometimes an undis-covered species of finch. Outside the church, post-service, the ladies would gather and curse the vulgar, brightly coloured shirts worn by the youths of the parish, clearly unaware that they themselves were sporting the most outstandingly ribald and gaudy headgear.

These 'church hats' were left on for a trip to the Max Jaffa performance – presumably as a mark of respect for the lord of the tea dance, as he tore through his repertoire of 'Daisy, Daisy' and 'On Mother Kelly's Doorstep' – and remained there for Sunday lunch followed by a stroll along the prom. On returning home that evening, the ladies would remove them and place them carefully back in the secure housing of their hatboxes, until the next Sunday. There were several accounts of their husbands creeping out of bed at night and approaching the hatboxes with shotguns, although the ladies would generally wrestle their spouses to the ground and remove the weapons before any damage could be inflicted.

Such everyday domestic shotgun dramas were nothing to the outlandish scenarios that were being concocted by my feverish imagination. I once became convinced for several weeks that I was an alien – planted on Earth as a test of my skills – and would shortly be taken back to my own planet by the scientists who deposited me on Earth.

I would often walk around staring straight ahead, knowing that certain people knew who and what I was, and that I had special powers, such as X-ray vision and super-hearing. I could also move about silently using the gift of tiptoeing and was adept in many forms of karate.

Mum and Dad ignored this, and I eventually gave up my conviction of alien origin in favour of the misguided belief that I was slowly being poisoned. I would question all foods presented to me with regard to the degree of arsenic that they contained. Mum would tell me not to be stupid but I continued with the questioning until one day she snapped and announced that, yes, my milk and biscuits contained a lethal amount of strychnine. I erupted into a sobbing wreck and never asked whether I was being poisoned again.

As if I were being punished for these fanciful imaginings, I fell ill, at the tender age of eight, with a flu-like condition that rendered me incapable and bedbound. I have little recollection of this time except the hallucinations I had whilst Mum mopped my fevered brow. These were on a par with some terrifying horror flick, a cross between *The Exorcist* and *Cinderella*, as Mum turned into a broom and danced about my bedchamber and I was chased by African wildlife onto a precipice.

A doctor was called. It was announced that I was suffering from the flu and treatment was administered. The truth was that I had consumption. I sweated and moaned for two weeks and eventually rose from my bed weak but healthy – still unaware of the potentially fatal sickness I had just encountered. It was only years later, when I had the jabs at school and the nurse asked whether I had been gravely ill in the past, that it was discovered that I could easily have perished from the killer TB.

Following my bout of illness I stayed at home, annoying Mum with my constant attempts to whistle. Mum was an expert whistler and I was envious both of her and of the industrialised trilling of the men who cycled past the house on their way to work. I needed to acquire this skill and wandered around the house blowing and hissing, but to no avail. My frustration was driving not just me but everyone else mad too, and one morning Mum snapped. I was ordered to leave the house and go into the fields, and not return until I had learned how to whistle.

There I stood, alone in the middle of a ploughed field, huffing and puffing for what seemed like hours until there emerged a thin squeal from between my pursed lips. I persevered and produced more shrill hoots until I had satisfied myself that I was a novice whistler with rudimentary, yet distinctly audible, skills. I rushed home and presented Mum with my crude and unsophisticated version of 'Colonel Bogie'. It was received with thanks and a round of applause, and I marched up and down the street demonstrating my new-found gift to anyone who would listen.

Outside of whistling practice, I spent a great deal of time out in the fields and woods – usually alone, and always having not the faintest idea of the time. In order to get a clearer view of the surrounding parishes, I was generally found roosting high in the branches of a tree. I would sit there for hours, silently monitoring the comings and goings of the sheep, farmers and ramblers, all of whom were completely unaware of my treetop vigil.

Once, while I had completely lost track of time on one of these lofty covert surveillance missions, Mum began to panic. She had searched the neighbourhood without success, and considered calling the police and a search party. This threat of search parties was a frequent warning – whether a search party was ever dispatched I entirely doubt, and it never discouraged me from forgetting the time.

These lapses in timekeeping were never malicious, I simply drifted off into a world of my own. On this particular occasion, I was discovered perching high in the upper branches of a poplar tree on the edge of a park – easily 500 feet above ground level, balanced ninja-like on a slender branch.

Mum unleashed a chilling scream followed by a stern injunction to, 'Get down from there before you fall.' I snapped out of my reverie and prepared to descend. This was always the problem – ascending trees was easy, descending was an arduous and demanding task, and on this occasion it appeared even more taxing.

In my haste to climb down the tree, I missed my footing on a branch and plunged through the leaves to my doom. There was another scream from Mum, but happily I caught hold of a passing stem, swinging round and through the tree like an enraptured gibbon, and eventually landed at her feet, just in time for a clip round the head and a severe bollocking.

It's strange to think that I spent so much of my time fearlessly aloft in precarious situations, as nowadays I suffer terribly from vertigo – to the point that I would gladly hurl myself from any tower given the opportunity
(one of the worrying aspects of vertigo and the reason I avoid such positions).

My final arboreal dance with death occurred when I decided to leap from a branch on one side of a tree to a branch on the other. This was, of course, impossible – unless I could leap around in the air. It had never been achieved yet, but there was always a first time, so I gave it a shot, and lo and behold, I fell – winded – onto the floor with my head just inches away from a pitchfork. I decided there and then that enough was enough: my tree climbing days were over.

CHAPTER
FIVE

'There's one in every school, and in mine she was called Eileen Macintosh'

There's one in every school, and in mine she was called Eileen Macintosh. That's not her real name, even though I do remember it ... but don't worry, Susan Griggs, my lips are sealed. (That's not her real name either – I'll leave it there.)

'Show me yours and I'll show you mine,' came the offer from within the doorway of the rear entrance to the school. She was of course referring to her private quarters, and the proposal went out to any passing boy willing to go along with this mutual exchange. I hasten to add that I was not one of these boys. In fact, she didn't have many takers at all, and could generally be found hovering around the doorway, proffering an individual viewing to each new passer-by, in a tone of increasing desperation.

I did, however, in the corner of an empty classroom, happen across a sight that remains with me to this day. Eileen had presumably recommended an inspection of her backstage area to a boy named (rather appropriately) Richard Boxman, who had agreed without reservation and was in the process of making his investigations when I entered the room and caught them at it – she crouching, bent double, he scrutinising her crevice with a pencil.

He turned and saw me, a look of desperation on his face, then returned to his work and — with the skills of an artisan — gently removed the pencil from the aperture and rose from his position. Eileen quickly arranged herself and sped out of the classroom. Richard calmly stepped towards me — his face now emotionless and vacant. As he approached, he raised the investigative pencil to my face and stood there for what seemed like an eternity.

What was he going to do with the filthy wand? I froze, staring at it, then — suddenly — he too made good his escape. It was a warning. If I revealed their secret, God knows what he would have done with the pencil. He probably still has that HB and now, if he reads this, he'll come after me with it. A further incident occurred a couple of years later, when a few of us were building a den on some wasteland. Planks had been nailed to trees and the interior decoration completed to the satisfaction of all concerned. This was the palace of the realm that was our wasteland kingdom, and we needed a king and queen. I opted to forgo the former honour in favour of a military role such as commander in chief of the army which — if we took a king out of the equation — meant that I was in charge of a fighting force of two, which was fair enough.

Brian Mitchell was the king, as decreed by himself, and my first assignment was to bring him a queen while he rested in his apartments. So off I went with my small army to find the king's consort. It wasn't long before one of my officers spotted a group of potential sovereigns, sitting on a wall throwing dough balls at a terrier.

'Would any of you girls fancy being the queen?' I enquired.

'Yes, me,' came the reply from — oh, no — Eileen Macintosh.

She didn't recognise me as far as I could tell, but I wasn't going to mention the pencil incident for fear of suggested involvement, so it was agreed that she would be taken back to the kingdom, escorted by her maids of honour.

We had decided to deliver the new monarch in style by carrying her to the palace on top of a sheet of corrugated iron sheeting. I – being the highest in rank – led the procession, and we raised her above our heads and commenced the sombre march towards the waiting king. As we neared our destination, I became aware of a cooling sensation on the back of my neck, followed by a downpour: it was Eileen Macintosh's piss.

She had relieved herself on this most solemn of occasions. She had spent a penny on board the royal corrugated iron. Perhaps it was the gravity of the event that had caused her to free herself, but I doubted it. I knew what she was about, and there was more to it than met the eye – my eye in particular, and hair, and neck, and back.

'Get off, you cow,' I howled, and hurled her to the ground. 'You dirty pig, you've wee'd on me – clear off and don't bother coming back.' She and her courtiers ran off giggling, while I tendered my resignation to the king and went home to cleanse myself physically and mentally.

I presume Eileen Macintosh went on to become involved in some form of sexual deviancy – bondage-mistress, sex slave-trader, or local government.

*

By this time, I was becoming more and more interested in music and pop stars, and the stranger they appeared and sounded, the more I liked them. Grandma had a radiogram that we could listen to but her choice of music was far removed from mine.

Endless repeats of *Oklahoma!* and *The Sound of Music* and Aunty Ada's Harry Secombe records did not 'switch me on'. A concession for Lois and me was a multi-coloured Pinky and Perky disc that filled me with horror and revulsion as I listened to these tormented pigs perform 'When the Red Red Robin Goes Bob-Bob-Bobbing Along', and a nightmarish interpretation of The Beatles' 'She Loves You'.

The visual image of these repulsive swine was bad enough, but their voices destroyed me – their insipid mewling and squealing left me begging for the disc to be removed and sawn in half or taken to the nearest veldt, where it could be trampled on by the next herd of stampeding wildebeest. In an attempt to discover who was behind this travesty of music, I would play the record at 33rpm and slow the voices down to reveal the identity of the culprits. This I did, and the puzzle was solved.

The true voices behind these loathsome porkers were none other than Matt Monro and Sammy Davis Jr. I vowed to have them shot as soon as finances permitted the hiring of a sniper. Sadly, this never happened, and Pinky and Perky went on to record many more nauseating songs, as well as being an enormous influence on the Bee Gees.

At home on Thursday evenings, I would be found stood beside the television miming to the turns on *Top of the Pops* for the benefit of the family – my favourite being an impersonation of Mick Jagger as he ran through 'Get Off Of My Cloud'. The lyrics were literally transposed into me, bidding Mum, Dad and Lois to remove themselves from my aerial platform before I got cross, while attempting to mouth the words with my tongue forced up over my top lip in a Jagger-like way. I also seem to recall me repeating this performance entirely nude in my bedroom window to entertain the cycling whistlers on their way home from work, although this may simply have been wishful thinking.

My constant requests for a record-player were rewarded one day when Dad brought home a Dansette – a tiny portable player not much bigger than a shoe box. When the volume was increased over halfway, your music would be accompanied by an invigorating hum.

We also had a record, The World of Val Doonican, and whatever world Val Doonican dwelt in, he could stay there without inviting me into it. Apparently he lived there with Paddy McGinty's goat and various other Irish halfwits intent on winning races at some distant Hibernian chutney fayre. Yet I couldn't help but have a faint fondness for Val as he gazed wistfully out of his LP sleeve at me, wearing the Fair Isle jumper that his Aunty Maggie from County Kilcraggy had knitted him.

I was still unsure as to which type of music I should adopt as my own. On a recent holiday to my cousins' in Bristol and following the 1966 World Cup, we had celebrated England's victory by holding our own football tournament in the field behind their house. My cousin Tim decided that the teams should be decided by who was a mod and who was a rocker.

'How do I know which I am?' I furtively enquired, so as not to look uncool.

'Do you like reggae?' asked Tim.

'What's that?' I queried.

'It's like Herman's Hermits,' was his explanation,

'Yes, I do like Herman's Hermits,' I replied, and sang, 'No milk today, the milkman's gone away.'

'Right then,' announced Tim, 'you're a mod,' and it was as simple as that. I had easily passed the introductory examination and I was now a confirmed mod, even though Herman's Hermits were actually about as moddish as Val Doonican.

Back at home and after a period of begging for a record of my own, I became the proud owner of The Wonderful World of Reggae. And it was a wonderful world – much better than Val Doonican's – this world was filled with mysterious rhythms and tales of Israelites and Monkey Spanners, skanking and ranking hot potatoes.

I had no idea what they were on about, but that made it all the more exciting. I played it over and over until it disappeared into a pile of dust. I was hungry for more music, but I wanted something different, I needed something even stranger than reggae, but where would I find it?

Hand in hand with music, went fashion. By 1966 I was becoming aware sartorially. When out of school, I wore a checked-tweed sports jacket almost permanently, and I had an impression of myself as a young Prince Charles, wearing fawn corduroy slacks and firm but fair shoes.

My hair was still formed into a floppy bowl-cut style with a round neck. The alternative 'neck' was a Roger Moore, or a 'Saint'. This was square in shape and favoured by more debonair characters than I. But longer hair was the way forward, and I wanted it. I began to pull my hair in a vain attempt to lengthen it, and when this failed I started to push hair in front of my ears into the shape of wings, as I had seen on pictures of the Small Faces.

This was accompanied by valiant efforts to develop a centre-parting, a goal which was partially achieved, enabling me to swagger around with the head of Little Lord Fauntleroy on the body of a 40-year-old geography teacher. Something had to change. The answer was Levi Strauss jeans and baseball boots. This was groovy fashion as well as play-wear, and served me faithfully for many years, with a duffle coat providing an extra layer of outer protection on cold winter's days.

There were, of course, occasional aberrations from the general rule of timeless elegance. One such oddity was the Clark's water-polished patent leather slip-on loafer – an item of footwear that (as its name suggests) could be polished with water to the high lustre of patent leather. These shoes were, I believe, formed from some kind of pliant resin expressly designed to expunge any vestige of breathability, and therefore guaranteed to seal in sweat and encourage mould growth on young feet.

They were also great fun, and boys who didn't possess a pair could often be found in the school toilets, begging the custodians of these futuristic slippers to be allowed to polish them. The pleasure of ownership was intense, but sadly it lasted only a few weeks before the shoes began to dissolve.

It was not long after this that flares arrived, and mother's seamstressing expertise was called into service to sew elongated triangular patches into straight-leg trousers and jeans. Mum was an expert with the needle and thread and regularly made us clothes. She was more than happy to insert excess material into the side of my trousers, but she went one better and got me to do it myself. This I did happily, and was thereby inducted into the magical worlds of embroidery and patch-sewing – skills which would stand me in good stead, in ways which I will return to later.

A school discotheque at around this time required a dynamic new outfit with which to impress my school-friends, and, after studying various designs from *FAB 208* and Mum's sewing patterns, I decided a pair of purple-flared hipsters would fit the bill. These were duly tailored to order, and accompanied by a mauve three-button grandad vest and a pair of new Chelsea boots that could double up as winter footwear for school.

The night of the dance arrived, and I looked fabulous. I burst through the double doors into the assembly hall, bristling with self-confidence, positioned myself so as everyone could admire my sensational new clobber, and was rewarded with rapturous indifference. Not to be thwarted in my moment of trend-setting, I began to leap around like an ape – kicking my legs out and striking star poses until, with one violent leg jerk, the crotch split on my hipsters.

That got the attention I required. Children gathered round and howled with laughter, mimicking my trouser-splitting movements and pointing fingers of ridicule at me. I responded with a repeat performance and a great night was had by all.

Incidentally, my Chelsea-cum-winter-school boots turned out to have soles that were made out of rice paper and wore through that very evening. On returning them to the shoe shop with an irate Mum in the vanguard, the shop assistant threw them back in our faces with a curt, 'It's the fashion.'

*

Aside from sartorial elegance and music, at the age of eight, my chief diversion and consuming passion was model aircraft – primarily Second World War planes. This obsession began at Christmas 1966 when I received an Airfix Trident as a present. I was overjoyed and set to work building it, with assistance from Dad, and proudly displayed it in my bedroom.

But this was only the start of it. From then on, all pocket money and payments received for menial tasks were saved in order to buy more and more models, 1/72 scale Focke Wulfs, Mitsubishi Zeros, Avro Lancasters and Grumman Avengers, and for birthdays, the more expensive 1/32 scale kits – a Messerschmitt 109 and the obligatory Spitfire.

I had a particular fondness for the Fleet Air Arm or sea planes, perhaps because Dad had been stationed on an aircraft carrier – HMS *Queen* – during the war, and via his stories I could relate to them more easily. Especially tales of flying over Russia lying in the belly of a Grumman Avenger and seeing the strange and beautiful narwhals in the Arctic. (Narwhals aren't aeroplanes, by the way, but white whales with ten-foot spears sticking out of their noses, like huge, fat marine unicorns, so this saga also fed my second passion – natural history.)

My partner in this love of aircraft was a freckle-faced and sandy-haired boy named Peter Shackleton. Mum always said that he looked like a First World War soldier, and she could see him in a previous life struggling through the Somme with a bandaged leg, like an escapee from a Wilfred Owen poem. It was true, he did have the look of yesteryear, a kind of Boy's Own quality – Tom Brown with a touch of G.K. Chesterton – and I admired this in him.

We would retreat into each other's bedroom sanctuaries and

discuss the merits of various planes, trying to outdo one another with mind-numbing facts like, 'How many exhaust pipes were there on the Spitfire mark 16?' and, 'What type of camouflage would be found on a Junkers Ju 88 if it were active in the desert theatre?'

We were also in competition as to how many models we had. Peter always had more than me, but I would out-manoeuvre him by building hybrids. I would take a kit of, let's say, a Heinkel 111, and attach the wings of an Avro Manchester and declare that it was a rare type that never saw service. His knowledge and expertise always saw through these scams, but he admired my skills at subterfuge.

As our collections increased to the point that we had almost a hundred kits between us, and our proficiency at making them grew greater, some of our earlier attempts became embarrassing. What should we do with these poorly constructed efforts? The answer was obvious: we would pack them full of gunpowder removed from fireworks saved from bonfire night and stage a mighty attack on them using fuses to ignite the planes as they sat sleepily on a makeshift airfield.

After careful consideration of a number of potential sites for this drama, we decided on the car park of the cash-and-carry near to Peter's house, and the stage was set for Sunday morning. Twenty aircraft were loaded with explosives, the fuses set and joined at a single ignition point.

The build-up to the annihilation of these innocent warplanes was provided by way of a commentary based on war films and comic books. Phrases like 'Hun in the sun at 12 o'clock', 'She's all yours, Ginger', 'Tail-end Charlie's bought it', 'Banzai!', 'Tora,

Tora, Tora', '*Gott im Himmel*', 'Take that, Fritz', 'FC's gone for a burton' and 'Dive, Dive, Dive' were bandied about indiscriminately until it was time to light the fuse.

*

The snaking paper ribbon was lit with a box of matches that Peter had smuggled out of his house and Boom! they all went up. It didn't turn out quite how we had imagined it – like an attack on an airfield in a Technicolor Panavision Battle of Britain film, with bombs and ack-ack going off at regular intervals over a period – but more of a single, all-consuming ball of fire, accompanied by a loud hissing sound and the smell of burning tar.

We stood agog and dismayed as we scanned this messy panorama of boiling plastic and glue, slowly realising that the heat from the fire had ignited the Tarmac. How could we douse this inferno? Blowing on it just increased its intensity, and weeing on it had no effect whatsoever. The only thing to do was run, and run we did – pausing only to bury the matches – vital evidence and deeply incriminating.

Half an hour later, hiding in the bushes, we saw the arrival of the fire brigade, who swiftly extinguished the blaze, leaving a scorch mark on the surface of the car park. We had convinced ourselves that there would be a major investigation into this case of wanton arson on a blameless section of Tarmac, and that Scotland Yard would be on the scene within minutes to take fingerprints from the charred remains of the models. We made a pact of silence and our alibis were that we were at the swings and knew nothing: in fact, we didn't even know where the cash-and-carry was.

That should stand up in court and save us from a life sentence. We thought it best if we stayed apart for a while, returned to our respective homes and acted like good boys – doing the washing-up, mowing the lawn and being general goody-goodies for a week until the Yard had forgotten about it and moved on to more important matters, like somebody writing 'Tits' on the side of a bus shelter, or a potato being rammed up someone's exhaust pipe.

A week later, we attached a string from Peter's bedroom window to the washing pole at the end of his garden, hung a Lancaster bomber from it and slid it down a couple of times. It would look a lot better if it blew up halfway down, we agreed. But by this point we had learnt our lesson that in pyrotechnic matters discretion is often the better part of valour.

Peter Shackleton and I remained great friends throughout our time at primary school, until his family moved away to Peterlee. Before he left, we stayed up all night at his house, watching Neil Armstrong and Buzz Aldrin land on the Moon. We sat in our pyjamas marvelling at the unfolding events, a bowl of cornflakes balanced on our laps, and a spoon hovering halfway between bowl and mouth as the Eagle landed, and we saw the future – a future that saw us living in Moon bases and travelling to work by jet-pack. We resolved to stay in touch and, when we had grown up, meet on a cloud base and show each other our model aeroplanes. Sadly, this happy reunion has yet to take place.

*

What with the conflicting demands of music, fashion and model aeroplanes, formal education was some way from the top of my agenda. Accordingly, my school reports from 1966 to 1970 display a steady accumulation of 'fairly goods' and an overall view that I was 'easily distracted'.

In July 1966, aged seven years and six months, my teacher, Miss Duncan, wrote that I was 'quickly distracted ... English subjects are quite satisfactory, but number [sic] needs careful attention'. The subjects I tended to do better at were English, history, art and nature study – which goes to show that nothing changes, as these are the same things I am interested in now. To the remainder of the curriculum – lessons like maths, physical and religious education, and science – I paid very little regard, spending most of the time entertaining my peers with diverting facial acrobatics and simple but effective sketches of bottoms.

One of my favourite methods of gaining respect from my class-mates was a masterful contrivance of illusion. We sat at double wooden desks complete with inkpots and a hole in the base of the desk. For what reason these holes existed, I had no idea. Perhaps it was to release ink that had overflowed from the pots and could be expelled in torrents onto our sandals like a sewage overflow, but as these inkpots were the size of a small eggcup that hypothesis had to be discounted. They may also have been there to discharge a build-up of gases collected from egg sandwiches and decaying fruit – or a pair of socks or underpants that had been left to rot over a term – but this too was highly unlikely.

The only reason I could find for the existence of these holes was to enable schoolchildren to practise the art of illusion. So I made a small nest of paper around the aperture and poked my finger through it from below, alerting my colleague that I had heard on good authority that something was living within the desk. On opening the lid and beckoning them to peer inside I would waggle my finger and inform them that it was a worm. This generally resulted in laughter on their part and mine, and culminated in the teacher making enquiries as to the source of this levity.

Without fail, I was shopped by my co-pilot. 'He's got a worm in his desk,' they would cry, eliciting from an irked master the following response: 'Well, let's take a look at this creature, I'm sure it's worth disrupting the class for.' I would then be forced to repeat my farcical performance for the benefit of the teacher and the rest of the class, this time to much lesser effect. 'We'll discuss this after school, Moir,' was generally the verdict that ensued, and I'd spend the rest of the day trying to think of a valid explanation – usually to no avail.

In 1968, it was remarked that 'greater effort would bring improvement all round', although, to my credit, I was 'a lively, active member of the class'. There being 45 pupils in our classroom meant that I had an enormous audience to impress, and facial gymnastics were becoming less effective, so I turned to sounds as a way of expressing my individuality – favourites being high- or low-pitched hums that the teachers could not accurately home in on. Various whirrs, clicks and buzzes were also employed, but again, I was always grassed up and would have to justify my wordless utterances to an increasingly worried teacher.

My shenanigans reached a climax in 1970, while being taught by Mr Dixon – an ex-World War Two flying ace who had flown Blenheim bombers on numerous sorties. I liked Mr Dixon a lot. He would thrill us boys with his tales of aerial combat. He looked

the part with his red hair and handlebar moustache, and the way
he spoke in his clipped, Brylcreem boy, chocks away lingo, he was
a cross between Terry-Thomas and the old Jimmy Edwards character of the headmaster in *Whacko*.

Mr Dixon carried with him a briefcase embossed with his
name, followed by DFC, signifying the Distinguished Flying
Cross, and it was this that earned me my first slippering. When it
came to discipline, Mr Dixon was from the old school. He wasn't
a tyrant by any means, but he was strict and believed in a firm
hand – and slipper. The cane was reserved for the headmaster's
correctional booth, but the slipper – a size 11 pre-war plimsole
– was terrifying enough.

On this occasion, my friend Alan Ianson had asked Mr Dixon
whether the DFC on his case stood for Darlington Football Club.
Alan knew perfectly well what it stood for, as did we all, but I
found this hilarious and we rolled about laughing as Mr Dixon's
face grew redder than his hair, until he boiled over in a passionate
fury that all but lifted the roof off the classroom.

'I fought the war so ungrateful little twerps like you could
attend schools like this. How dare you insult not only me but the
entire Royal Air Force and your country. Step up here, you boys.'

We silently made our way to the front of the room.

'Over,' he bellowed. 'You first, Ianson. You shall receive six
strikes, and if you should decide to rise before I have administered them, we shall start again at the beginning.'

I stood by and watched my pal's face as he was slugged with the
giant shoe, with the sad knowledge that I was next. Unfortunately
for Alan, after five bats he could take no more and rose from his
position with a tearful yelp, and it was back to the beginning.

Eleven strikes of the slipper. 'No thanks,' I thought. 'I shall receive six with thanks. I shall not rise from my prone position, let the punishment begin.' And so it did.

'Touch your toes, Moir.' I did, and awaited the first blow, and it came with the velocity of W.G. Grace hitting a six at Lords. The pain reverberated through my body and into my mind. I suspect that Mr Dixon was very likely a top cricketer and the practice was welcome. I took my punishment as stoically as I could and returned to my seat and sat, buttocks on hands, in an attempt to allow air to the boiling flesh, stifling tears and trying to look as nonchalant as possible.

Mr Dixon had a rather large nose and protruding from its tip was a long russet hair – at a guess, about two inches long, and well known to the class. On one occasion, a science lesson involved conducting experiments in smell and taste. We were to hold our noses, close our eyes, and place a mystery piece of food in our mouths, the object being that if you held your nose you couldn't taste the food.

Mr Dixon demonstrated this in front of us. Amid a tight group of intrigued children, he shut his eyes, held closed his bulging proboscis, and slowly delivered a piece of carrot into his open mouth. The hair was on full display – erect and proud. I seized the opportunity of a lifetime, quickly grabbed a pair of scissors from a nearby desk and – while his eyes were closed – snipped it off.

When would I ever learn? As soon as the deed was done the entire group erupted into thunderous laughter.

'Who pruned my aerial?' or some such cry, roared the master.

'Him, him!' they pointed, and I stood undone, guilty as

charged, still holding the scissors and the hair lying forlornly on the floor between us.

Once again, I was to receive the brutal disbursement of the slipper. This time, I swiftly, and with great stealth, slipped an exercise book down the back of my trousers. I took my position in front of my accusers to learn that the punishment for nose-hair trimming was twelve brushes of the mammoth footwear. This was increased to thirteen when the concealed book was discovered.

I remained doubled over as the judgment was meted out and this time, on returning to my seat, I could not disguise my anguish. I raised the lid of my desk and filled it with tears, and as I wept gallons of pain-filled droplets, I saw through the misty haze to the hole at the bottom of the desk. The mystery was solved. That was what it was for: to allow the tears of recently beaten children to escape, so as not to dampen and destroy their coursework.

CHAPTER
SIX

'I was under the impression that it was a lead guitar in the sense of the heavy soft metallic element'

My sister Lois was three years younger than me and almost directly opposite in temperament – she being quiet, diffident and home-loving, although she played the stooge well to my comedic lead.

I would spend mealtimes pulling extraordinary and distorted faces at her until she exploded with laughter, scattering her mouthful of food about the table. On questioning from parents as to the meaning of this hilarity, Lois would point at me and I would shrug and offer my arms up in the time-honoured 'I don't know what she's talking about' manner.

Another form of amusement for which Lois was employed was as a human canvas for my artistic endeavours. I would position her prostrate on the sitting-room floor and, with her lying upside down and away from me, begin to sketch on her forehead. Above her eyes, I would draw a nose with my biro and beneath it a mouth, leaving her upside-down eyes to form a grotesque and hilarious face. Her real nose and mouth would be covered with a flannel or some similar cloth, leaving me to sit back and giggle at the finished product. You might like to try this at home on a sibling, spouse or parent – it really is worth the effort.

It wasn't only a sketchboard I used Lois for, I also used her as a critic for my artwork. On one occasion this led to trouble.

We were staying at Grandma and Aunty Ada's house in Leeds, where Lois and I slept on a lilo in the spare bedroom. One evening, when we were dispatched to bed I decided to give Lois a lesson in biology, in the form of two diagrams of a man and a woman disrobed and displaying their private portions.

Being aged nine, I was becoming aware of the various differences between the sexes, and thought that I should impart this knowledge to my younger and more naive sister. 'This is a lady's bosoms,' I announced, pointing at the 'W' shape with two dots jabbed into the 'U' bends, 'and this is the other place,' I indicated, emphasising the crudely drawn triangulation station beneath.

'And here on the gentleman,' I continued, in my best lecturer's voice, 'is his willy and dangly bits, which are used for weeing. The difference between men and women is that the men can wee upwards, and sometimes over walls. This makes men better than women, and there ends today's lesson.' Lois appeared suitably unimpressed, so I stuffed the diagrams under the lilo and went to sleep.

The following day, as we drove home, Dad was in a particularly pensive mood. Driving along a long and uneventful stretch of road, he suddenly swerved into a lay-by in the middle of nowhere and switched the engine off. After an ominous period of silence, he slowly turned to me in the back seat and displayed the crude medical diagrams.

'What are these?' he solemnly enquired.

I was rooted out and brought directly into disrepute before the family. There was no escape. I could not blame Lois, nor

Grandma. There was only one hope if I was to worm my way out of this shabby hole, and I played my only card. 'It was Aunty Ada – she drew that.'

'No, she didn't. You know very well that you drew this, and it will never happen again, do you understand?'

'Yes,' I murmured ashamedly – head bowed, and tears beginning to well. We drove home in silence, the sketches now firmly housed in the glove compartment, yet somehow burning a hole through the wood into my watery eyes. What would happen to them?

Would they be shown to the rest of the family, friends and relatives as a warning to other potentially sick-minded offspring? Would they be published in the *Northern Echo* with my pathetic face next to them? Or, even worse, would it be revealed that I had attempted to blacken the name of Aunty Ada? Her wrath was unimaginable. I vowed there and then never to attempt biological drawings again, which I didn't ... at least not until the following week.

*

On Thursday afternoons, Mum would collect Lois and me from school and we would catch the number 1 bus downtown to the civic library and art gallery. Mum was taking evening classes at art school and was very good – especially at watercolours and pottery – and we would begin our trips with a stroll around the paintings and sculptures. In fact, one of these trips was documented by the *Northern Echo* with a photograph of me, aged nine, and Lois, seven, gazing unexcitedly and with undisguised apathy at a painting of a yacht by a nameless child from Aycliffe School.

Following the dash around the art gallery (a habit I have retained when visiting art museums – I tear through the rooms like a man on fire, drinking in the works as curators unholster their revolvers, assuming I am carrying a Kandinsky beneath my Pac-a-mac), we would repair to the junior library. There I would head straight for the natural history section and select my week's reading.

I was allowed to take out three books a week on my pale blue card, and by the age of ten, I had exhausted the children's shelves and was hungry to enter the sophisticated world of the adult library. This was a veritable labyrinth with its high stacks of books. And the room was alive with the smell of dust, damp, woollen topcoats and the specific regional odour of oil, coolant and Swarfega (impregnated into not only the overalls of the men but their skin as well), all topped off with a generous coating of Brylcreem, and the whole miasma drenched in a sickly cheap cologne bought from a stall in the open market in a doomed attempt to disguise the fetid honk.

The day I was awarded my adult library card was a great day: I was one step nearer to becoming a man. Forget dropped testicles, voice adjustments and excess fur growth, I was now permitted to withdraw books of an adult nature, and I did ... the first selection to go home with me was *Gray's Anatomy* and Darwin's *The Origin of Species*. Thank goodness I also chose *White Fang* by Jack London.

Mum always picked out choice historical novels, especially favouring the works of Philippa Gregory and, eventually, because of her interest, so did I. In fact, to this day we read and swap books of this genre – isn't that lovely?

*

Like other boys of my age, I would spend the evenings after school playing over the fields, bird-nesting and kicking balls at trees, or digging deep holes and burying soil in them. But I would always leave for home early on Thursday nights so as to catch *Top of the Pops* – usually to cries of, 'You're only going to watch it to see Pan's People, you poof.' How I warranted the title of 'poof' by allegedly going off to watch some semi-naked girls frolicking to the chart-bound sounds of the time, I don't know, but it wasn't them I was interested in, it was the music.

Likewise, on a Friday night I would vanish early from levering up a sapling or upturning a cattle trough and beating it with sticks until it took on a frightening aspect ... important work, I know, but I had equally important work at home. Friday night was rock night on Radio 1 with Annie Nightingale, and she played tracks by bands that weren't in the charts. It was by this means that I was introduced to the likes of Soft Machine, Elephant's Memory and Iron Butterfly performing 'Inna Gadda Vida'.

The title of that song was mysterious and weird, or so I thought. Years later I discovered that it was merely the guitarist and song-writer, after consuming several bottles of Jack Daniel's , attempting to tell the rest of the group that the title of his masterpiece was 'In the Garden of Eden', and through his slurred speech it transformed into 'Inna Gadda Vida'. I was still impressed, though.

I would listen to this music like an obsessed mullah, sucked into its weaving twists and turns, its coils and crescendos, and piecing together the obscure and riddle-filled lyrics with Annie's sage-like words in between records. And thus I became aware that I was not a mod, but a psychedelic, a hippy, a groover, a shaker, and very possibly a flower-child.

*

One day in 1969, I was out shopping with Mum and Dad in Darlington town centre. We had just emerged from Dresser's stationery and bookshop when I spied a white Daimler crawling along the High Row. As it passed by, I noticed a face I recognised peering out of the back window. It was Jimi Hendrix, my hero. I tore off in pursuit of the guitarist, battling against the overpoweringly rich aroma of patchouli oil and Strawberry Fields joss sticks that drifted through the slightly open window.

Having fought my way through the sweet miasma, I drew alongside the car and stared through the window. I had a million things I wanted to say to him, but amazement, exhaustion and a lungful of Asian perfume caused this to be transformed into a wide-eyed gawk accompanied by an inane grin and a little wave. He looked at me, smiled that charismatic smile, and waved back.

This was my first contact with a pop star and with somebody of whom I was a fan, and later that year I saw my first live pop group, Dave Dee, Dozy, Beaky, Mick and Tich at the pantomime at Stockton. While performing their hit 'Zabadack', Dave Dee wielded an enormous bullwhip that he cracked during the chorus in order to emphasise the gravity of his words, which no one could deny as they were in some invented foreign language that only Dave knew. A translation might have been something like, 'Zabadack, your government will fall unless you meet my outlandish demands', but I doubt it. Anyway, who would take a group seriously whose members had names like Dozy and Beaky? It simply wouldn't happen today – imagine a pop group like U2 with names like that … maybe that's not such a good comparison.

Anyway, I found out years later that on the evening of the day I encountered him, Hendrix performed at the Imperial Hotel bar, a tiny basement room with a stage the size of a small shed – and this at the height of his career. During the performance he rammed his guitar through the ceiling, which was made of square, perforated asbestos tiles, and continued to thrash it to within an inch of its life. I was shown this piece of rock memorabilia by the landlord and gawped at it in silence, in much the same way as I had years earlier at the man himself.

A year later, Jimi was dead. But I was still an obsessive fan, so much so that when *Sounds* music paper appeared with pull-out posters of Eric Clapton, Janis Joplin and Hendrix, I Sellotaped the Hendrix poster onto the inside of my wardrobe and began to use it as a dartboard. I saw no disrespect to the man in these actions – I still adored him – it was simply a good target. I even had a point-scoring system: one point for his body, five points for his guitar and ten points if I got him in the eyes.

My wardrobe-cum-dartboard was the focal point of my bedroom empire. I painted the outside Prussian blue and used the mirror on the front to hone my microphone-swinging technique using Grandad Leigh's old walking stick. Head thrust back, I would drop to my knees and wail along to the progressive and exciting sounds of the Annie Nightingale show. If there was a guitar solo, the walking stick would metamorphose into a Les Paul or a Stratocaster and even more curious poses would be struck as I played the stick through my legs, round the back of my head — all this accompanied by facial contortions akin to somebody being 'broken on the wheel' or some such medieval torture.

I would record *The Friday Rock Show* on a Ferguson tape recorder that Dad had bought for a couple of quid from someone at work, and while I was recording the tracks I would commentate over them, giving my opinion on the performances with observations such as, 'That was an excellent bass solo,' or, 'That's Leslie West there, on lead guitar.'

At this juncture, I must point out that having read music papers whenever I got the chance, I was under the impression that it was a lead guitar in the sense of the heavy soft metallic element and not because it was the prime instrument in the group. Accordingly I pronounced it 'led'.

Dad questioned me about this once and I scoffingly replied, 'No, Dad, it's a "led" guitar, because it plays heavy music.'

'Oh, well,' he replied patiently, 'you know best.'

These tapes may still exist. In fact I dearly hope that someone, somewhere may have the recordings of an excited young boy warbling enthusiastically over some tracks by Piblokto (Cream lyricist Pete Brown's spin-off band), expounding the virtues of a 'led' trumpet.

*

As well as being the date of my close encounter with Jimi Hendrix, 1969 was also space year. The excitement felt by myself and Peter Shackleton as we watched Apollo 11 dropping off Armstrong and Aldrin on the Moon was only the beginning. Space posters were given away free with cornflakes and Stanley Kubrick released *2001: A Space Odyssey* for us to wonder at.

I wondered long and hard at that. I saw it at the cinema and hadn't got a clue what it was all about, but I loved the way it looked – the baby floating through space, the monolith and the spaceship. The thing I loved about it most of all, however, was the music, and I put in a bid for the theme to become the first single I ever bought. I'd saved up some pocket money and Mum and Dad agreed to make up the difference, so off I strode with my 6s/11d to buy it.

As we were staying at Grandma's at the time, we headed for Leeds city centre to find a record shop, and so we did in one of the arcades. There it was in one of the racks – my first 45rpm single.

I was so eager – telling Mum all the way back to Grandma's what a great piece of music it was and how happy I was that I owned it – and finally, when we arrived, I made a beeline for the radiogram.

Tossing a Harry Secombe record aside, I carefully placed my new acquisition on the deck and gently dropped the needle onto the vinyl. What came out of the speakers wasn't the theme from *2001: A Space Odyssey* but some throttle-throated bloke wittering on about being trapped in his rocket. I ripped the single off the turntable and examined the label. David Bowie: 'Space Oddity'.

I had wasted my time and money, but – not to be outdone – I was determined to like this misunderstanding and played it endlessly. Three weeks later, 'Space Oddity' was in the Top Ten and I had owned it for ages, making me the coolest kid in school by default.

*

Soon there would be a new and more demanding constituency to be won over. In 1970, I left Eastbourne Junior School and prepared to join the heaving throng at Eastbourne Secondary, but first came the summer holidays – six weeks of joy, riding bikes into walls and building dens in the fields.

As my transfer to Eastbourne Secondary – or Big School as it was technically termed – drew nearer, my sense of anticipation grew. It was a combination of excitement and panic – excitement at the knowledge that I was embarking on the final stages towards becoming a man, and panic that there were probably boys there who had already grown into men and were no doubt capable of brutalising younger and more innocent individuals such as myself. I also felt some consternation at the prospect of being forced to grow up and 'put away childish things'. The latter eventuality, of course, I avoided. The former, you shall hear about later.

Summer holidays for the Moirs usually took the form of camping trips to the Lake District or the west coast of Scotland. These involved protracted rambles across mountain tops and valleys, punctuated by dips in icy streams and picnics eaten from red plastic plates with clip-together cutlery. I loved these holidays. Even though the hikes were sometimes punishing, there was a great sense of achievement about them which formed the basis of my later becoming a romantic aesthete (when it suited me).

The areas chosen for our camping holidays were, however, prone to diabolical weather, and downpours and gales regularly flushed us out of campsites and back home, where we would remain stoically satisfied with 'days out' for the remainder of the holiday. It was as a result of one of these truncated voyages in the summer of 1969 that the next year brought not one but two breaks with tradition.

*

Lois and I had been pestering Mum and Dad to take us to Butlin's Holiday Camp for a week. There was one situated in Filey on the North Yorkshire coast, and, after barraging them with pleas, we were granted our wish, and off we went. It looked like a disused aerodrome with bunkers and mess halls now used as accommodation. Everything about the place cried out 'Welcome, ladies and gentlemen, to 1955!' The *Hi-De-Hi* atmosphere permeated every artery of this concrete and plastic expanse, and we loved it.

We were housed in a small cabin with a predominantly rouge feel about it and outside we had a small patio on which we could consume our lemon barley water.

Every moment of the day there was some brilliant 1950s-style show presided over by an ageing teddy boy or a Freddy 'parrot face' Davies imitator, who, after a day's 'madcap' entertaining – jumping up and down and mak-ing various squawks, squeals and fart sounds – would retire to his berth and weep bucketloads into his nylon-sheeted pillowcase recalling his lost love – a moon-faced dulcimer player from Cardiff who abandoned him and fled to Jersey with a singing fitter named Bernie Caruso.

I travelled around the encampment tightly clutching a small red autograph book. I had already ensnared Jimmy Savile at a Golden Egg in Bridlington and commanded him to sign, and also the great Pat Phoenix as she arrived off a flight at Yeadon airport in Leeds.

She was very polite and kind and had a beehive hairdo that

defied gravity – several light aircraft were lodged in its upper storeys (although this was only rumoured, as the summit was hidden in the cloud-base).

Anyway, I was resolute in filling my book and hovered around the sides of stages awaiting the turns' and MCs' exit, ready to pounce on the unsuspecting entertainers and demand their signatures. In a day, I'd got a scrawl on every page from redcoats with names like Rollin' Ronnie, Pierre and Francois, The Amazing Dick, and an ancient organist who went by the name of Les, the King of the Zeppelins. What he meant by this I had no idea – presumably he shot down zeppelins in the First World War, rather than considering himself the chief player in Led Zep.

During one of my autograph-hunting forays I stumbled upon an afternoon teenage dancing competition. I was spied crouching behind one of the seats in the stalls by the host of the competition – a pretty, highly strung, blonde-haired girl of about eighteen, who beckoned me onto the stage. I crouched silently, hoping she would forget about me and select some other, more forthcoming youth, but seeing as there were only two other kids in the room, it was hard to escape her desperate clutches, and I was prised out from my position with a broom and forced to stand on the stage awaiting my instructions.

'Do you like dancing?' she enquired.

'No,' I dismally responded.

'Who's your favourite group?' she jovially wondered.

'The Thirteenth Floor Elevators,' I lied, knowing that she would never have heard of them.

'Oh, I like them too,' she said, 'but we haven't got them, so dance to "Sugar, Sugar" by The Archies.'

I was dumbstruck – this was a song sung by cartoon characters and definitely not fitting for a super-cool individual such as I.

I reluctantly shuffled about like a drunken mortician until the horrifying ordeal was over and then ran from the stage, nimbly side-stepping her before she could catch me and award a prize, thus requiring a repeat performance. I ran and ran until I found a safe haven in the boiler-house of the casino, where I tried to scrub the shame from my besmirched body.

Another activity I actively took no part in was the poolside beauty queen contests. Several plump and spotty girls, with corned-beef legs and hair that had been styled by blowlamp, shuffled along the boardwalk offering sickly smiles to a group of middle-aged men in blazers who examined them one by one, snorted and wrote down a figure.

Occasionally one of the men would bend down beneath the table and rise up again looking faintly guilty. I crept round to the side of the judges table to investigate. There beneath the table and under their chairs was a bottle of whisky. One judge would take a surreptitious swig and move the bottle with his foot along to his neighbour, whereupon it was his turn for a sly manoeuvre.

The girls would then have to justify their existence on Earth to these disinterested sots by way of a puritanical moralising speech in the style of a Quaker minister expounding the virtues of right-eousness and altruism. When this was over, the girls would run off to a redcoat's hut to be ravaged while gargling Babychams and puffing on Capstan Full Strengths.

*

Memories of the previous year's washout camping trip on the North Yorkshire moors led Mum and Dad to allocate the remainder of our hols to an extended visit to Aunty Rae, Uncle Norman and the cousins' house in Bristol. It was a large house – big enough to accommodate all of us, with the added luxury of a roof that wasn't canvas, and a location that ensured we could still go on our mammoth hikes around Cheddar Gorge and the Somerset Levels.

The bonus of taking trips to Bristol were playmates in the form of our cousins. Barb was twelve – only six months older than me. Tim was fourteen, and Pam – another three years older – was an adult as far as I was concerned, so not as much of a play pal as the other two.

Uncle Norman's job was to seek out artists whose work could be transformed into prints that could be sold in high streets at affordable prices for average wage-earners to hang above their fireplaces: paintings like ballet dancers performing *Swan Lake*, a Spitfire emerging from a fleecy white cloud, or a tea-trader returning home from the Indies on a tranquil sea.

There were rumours that Uncle Norman had discovered the artist responsible for the famous *Green Lady*: an oriental woman with green skin reclining on a log, looking pensively off-canvas – perhaps at one of her captors, or maybe at a gentleman caller with equally verdant skin, relaxing on a nearby log. This painting spawned hundreds of similar pictures of vibrantly coloured women relaxing in forestry or pinned against the walls of bamboo huts, gazing wistfully away with only the slightest degree of torment in their exotic eyes.

These images were a hangover from the 1950s and early 1960s

love of the luxuriantly foreign, and would be accompanied in sitting rooms by bamboo furniture, bongos, and ebony carvings of Masai warriors' heads. But by the beginning of the 1970s, the nation's fondness for vivid oriental beauties was giving way to a new vogue for monumentally disturbing portraits of weeping orphans in rags, desperately clutching a puppy or a tattered flannel.

Heaven knows what torments led to this degree of unhappiness, but people bought them and hung them on their walls. Quite often the depicted urchins had oversized heads (I'm not suggesting that they were suffering from water on the brain – although that wouldn't be a surprise) which was the final indignity, as, in the course of their infinite suffering, they had been transformed into semi-cartoon characters in order to elicit more sympathy from the viewer. In later years, these nauseating prints were finally condemned to the jumble sale in favour of the much more appealing image of the woman scratching her arse with a tennis racket, or the black-and-white photo of a young couple on a bridge in New York.

Anyway, Uncle Norman dealt exclusively in the tasteful end of this market, and on this particular holiday we accompanied him on one of his trips to Dartmouth, with a view to seeing an artist who had painted a picture of the ship from *The Onedin Line* – as far as I can remember, a TV period drama about a doleful sea captain struggling to meet the unreasonable demands of his employers. We were allowed on the set at the quayside and saw the filming in progress, and I began to record the scene with my new second-hand box Brownie camera (in fact it was Mum's old one from her teens).

I strolled about the set, snapping away at the various characters

My incredible bulk

Me in giant pram

OOH! EEEE!

AN EXAGERATED IMAGE OF THE INTERIOR OF A BOND MINICAR

The interior of the
Bond Minicar (page 22)

THE MOIRS IN PROGRESS

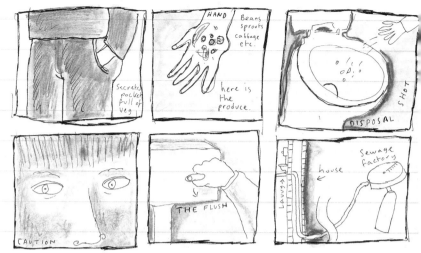

vegetable dumping procedure
(page 35)

Diagram of our lounge

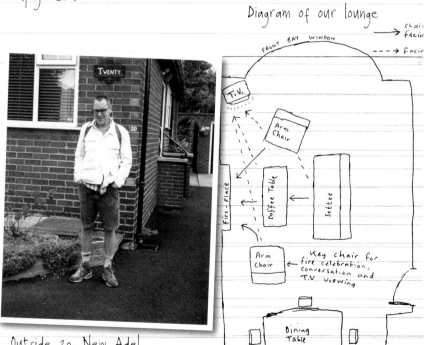

Outside 20, New Adel
Gardens

Above left: Me, Grampy and Lois

Above Right: With Dad in Scarborough

My ideal Crow (page 46)

My Ideal
CROW
circa: 1965

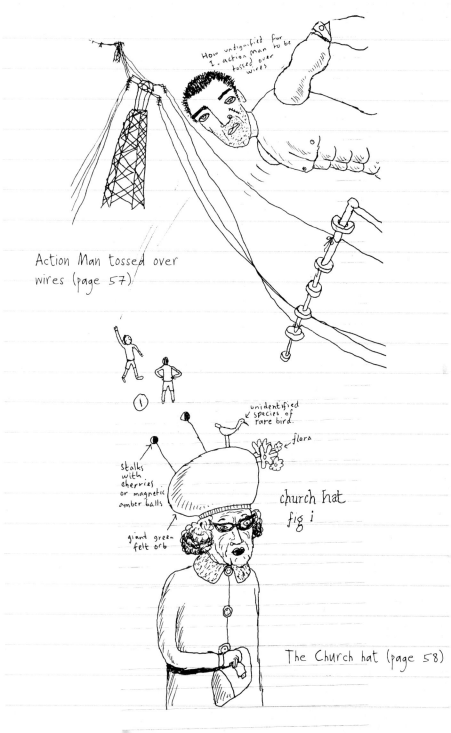

How undignified for I. action Man to be tossed over wires

Action Man tossed over wires (page 57)

①

unidentified species of rare bird.

flora

stalks with cherries or magnetic amber balls

church hat fig i

giant green felt orb

The Church hat (page 58)

Our planes, ready for
take-off (page 74)

Above: Making clay pots with
Lois
Left: Me and Hodgy
(page 101)

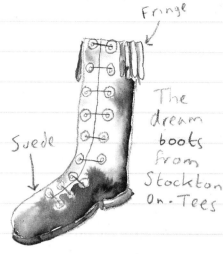

Fringe

Suede

The dream boots from Stockton-On-Tees

The dream boots
(page 128)

My scabby platforms
(page 129)

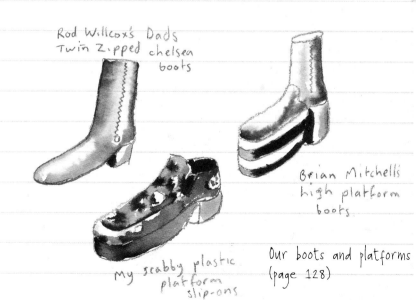

Rod Willcox's Dads Twin Zipped chelsea boots

My scabby plastic platform slip-ons

Brian Mitchell's high platform boots.

Our boots and platforms
(page 128)

The moronic sibling
(page 146)

Left: Piglet castration
(page 155)

Below: The Articulated Cart
(page 148)

fig.1

Giant Haystacks (page 161)

Simpleton setting fire to
costume (page 166)

Inside the ABC Cinema
(page 163)

and crew, until I was forcibly ejected from the quay for inter-
rupting filming. On processing, the looks of annoyance from the
filmers were quite clearly apparent. One in particular shows the
star of the show — Peter Gilmore — and the director of photog-
raphy looking as if they were moments from slitting my throat.

It was on this holiday that I was introduced to Led Zep II and
King Crimson, thanks to my sharing the attic bedroom with Tim.
I was blown away by Robert Plant's supersonic wailing, Bonzo's
meat-hammer drumming and Robert Fripp's extraordinary guitar
technique, and would play them over and over until I knew every
note. I would be armed with this knowledge when I started at my
new school. It would be a handy weapon when the time came to
make a first impression. I was ready to enter the world of the Big
Lads.

CHAPTER
SEVEN

'I had inadvertently begun big school with a camp haversack'

Eastbourne Secondary School was an imposing slab of Victorian austerity. Its unsmiling face announced that you were here to work under the gravest of conditions, and amusement should be left at the gate upon entering its puritanical environs. The school, so the stories went, used to be a hospice for the terminally ill. Its Victorian designers had presumably hoped to make the patients' final days as hopeless and gloomy as possible. Hence the high windows – not only were they a spur to melancholy, but they made it significantly more difficult for would-be suicides to hurl themselves to their deaths, thus prolonging their misery to its lengthiest degree.

Sports were performed in the 'walled field', a huge expanse of grass surrounded by a ten-foot wall, high enough to prevent the sick from escaping. In the centre of the school buildings was the quadrangle – a confined, cloister-like area, presumably once used to harrow the inmates into submission for the crime of contracting some corruption of the human body by way of sin. Whatever the reason for their ailments, they would suffer extensively here in order to secure a reasonable position at God's table in the near future.

Chapter Seven

My first day at Eastbourne began with Mum brushing my hair with extra ferocity, destroying my new centre-parting in favour of the old on-the-side variety, and driving the nylon-bristled brush firmly into my scalp to ensure that no amount of tomfoolery would lead to dishevelment. I felt manly in my new uniform of navy blue woollen jacket with the E.S. device on the breast pocket, light blue shirt, pale and dark blue striped tie, black trousers, and 'Wayfarer' shoes. These were the new shoe sensation for boys and featured animal track prints in relief on the sole, so you could ram your shoe into the mud next to an animal print and compare them until you had a match.

The problem was we didn't have many red deer or otters in our school, so the shoes were rarely used in any way other than for traditional footwear-type purposes. There was another special feature inside the shoe – a compass to help you decide which way an animal was travelling while you were tracking it. Sadly, even if I had wanted to use it in this way it would have been impossible, as the compass was rendered useless within days from condensation caused by sweaty feet.

All ready for school, I went and called for Steve Hodgson, who appeared as neat and groomed as me – his curly brown hair firmly brushed towards the west, in a style not too dissimilar to that later modelled by Douglas Hurd. Steve's mum took a photo of us to commemorate the occasion, and off we went to join the big lads.

On entering the quadrangle, we were herded into groups representing our new classes. I was in 1 Wa, the 'W' standing for the house I was in – Witton, named after a local castle (the others were Bolton, Durham and Richmond, if you were wondering).

The first new friend I made was Rod Willcox. Our amity seemed to be pre-destined by virtue of the fact that we both shared the same name. The initial conversation went something like this.

Rod W: Hello, my name's Rod.
Rod M: So's mine – that's strange, isn't it?
Rod W: I know, 'cos there's not many Rods around, is there?
Rod M: No, there's not, so we should be friends, then.
Rod W: Yes, we should ... what stuff do you like, then?
Rod M: Stuff that's funny, silly and daft.

And that was it. We were best friends from that moment on. Our catchphrase was 'funny, silly and daft', said in the style of Jimmy Clitheroe or a mentally challenged working men's club compere. This verbal formulation could be relied upon to reduce us to helpless fits of giggling in almost any situation, but it worked best when offered as a description of something quite serious and not funny in the slightest, for instance:

Rod M: What did you think of the solar eclipse?
Rod W: I thought it was funny, silly and daft.

This would cause us to roll around howling with laughter, while alienating the other kids who weren't in on the joke, causing them to treat Rod and me like the morons we presented ourselves to be. Not that we cared: it all added to the hilarity of the situation.

We also infuriated our peers, as well as teachers and parents, by speaking in the newsreaderly voice adopted by John Cleese on *Monty Python's Flying Circus* in his 'And now for something completely different' character.

Monty Python had been on our TV screens for a year by then and I was hooked. I thought it was hysterical, and not only that, it appeared not to be understood by adults, which made it even more appealing. Rod and I would invent our own *Python* sketches, which would begin with 'Wouldn't it be funny if ...', followed by two paradoxical situations presented in a deadpan way.

One instance was the following suggestion: 'Wouldn't it be funny if cancan dancers were glued to the stage and couldn't stand up? They would have to do the whole show lying down.' We would then demonstrate how funny this would be with a half-hour performance. Hardly the leading edge of comedy, but it was ours and it made us laugh and that was all that mattered.

*

One thing I knew about fitting in at big school was that in order to have even the tiniest amount of cool, you had to have your haversack flap painted. Please let me explain. A haversack is a regional, over-the-shoulder, canvas satchel-type bag, originally used for carrying 'havers' or oats, with a flap over the opening at the top. But in this case it was being used as a school bag.

I was aware that the flap had to display the name of a popular football team or pop group – something cool and hip and not, for instance, your own name, or the name of a charity like the RSPCA, although oblique references to company names such as ESSO or STP were admissible because of their link to the manly sport of motor racing. Freeman, Hardy & Willis would be unacceptable. Coca-Cola might just about creep in, but Lowcock's lemonade was a no-no. Cartoon characters were on the cusp, but they had to be old ones like Felix the Cat, Goofy or Popeye, and, if you were really cool, Fritz the Cat – the randy X-rated cartoon character that most kids had heard of, but hadn't seen, and teachers definitely didn't know about.

I decided to ease myself in gently with a football team. The problem was I had no interest in football and didn't support anyone in particular, so I asked cousin Barb, who was very sporty and knew about such arcane matters. Her suggestion was that I lionise Bristol Rovers, but I had a feeling that they weren't stylish enough.

I quite liked West Ham United for their colours – claret and sky blue, a marvellous combination: well done. Norwich presented themselves with a striking, vibrant, canary yellow: wonderful. But, after much deliberation, I decided on Everton – because I liked the sound of the name (presumably it reminded me of mints), and their blue and white combination was subtle yet dynamic.

Using Humbrol enamel paint, of which I had gallons for painting my models, I began work on the haversack by diagonally colouring the flap blue and white, with Everton written across it in bubble writing – the latest thing in hip calligraphy. This, of course, was an error that I should have spotted: football and groovy lettering don't mix. I had inadvertently begun big school with a camp haversack.

Fortunately, I realised this myself. Questions were raised before I could rectify the situation, but mainly regarding the team, and not my airy-fairy font, as I didn't know the names of any Everton players. This was turning into a disaster: my whole time at big school could become unbearable unless I did something about the bag, and quick.

The Everton haversack lasted only one day. That night, after my first day at school, I set to work on repainting the flap. This time I would get it right. Forget football, what did I like that was cool? Music. But who was hip enough to eulogise? Some group that nobody had heard of, but with a strange and groovy name.

I flicked through my copy of the *New Musical Express* and there it was, staring out at me – the first album by a new group called Black Sabbath. I copied the typeface perfectly in silver on a purple background and proudly marched back into school, safe in the knowledge that I was carrying a mysterious emblem.

The Black Sabbath image remained there for a while, until I heard Alice Cooper on the radio one night, performing 'Seventeen'. Alice Cooper was still relatively unknown at this stage and thus a perfect candidate for my perplexing paintwork. So I set to work, copying from a monochromatic image of Cooper I found, once again, in the *NME*. The image portrayed him topless and wearing gravity-defying hipsters, his long hair flowing over his shoulders.

Artwork complete, I strode back into school, proudly swinging my bag from side to side for all to see. Within seconds I was pounced on by Mr Bryant, the headmaster. 'What is the meaning of this, boy?' he screamed, causing the entire school to drop whatever they were doing and gather around me to see what the fuss was about. 'You have a painting of a naked woman on your haversack, that is unacceptable,' he continued.

'It's not a woman, sir,' I whimpered in response.

'Do you think I'm stupid, boy? I can clearly see her nipples, you disgusting object, and you've even written her name there – Alice Cooper, whoever that may be. Is she a stripper, you young pervert?'

'Sir, it's a man and he's a rock singer.'

'It's a picture of a naked woman, boy. Has anybody else here heard of this revolting person, Alice Cooper?'

'No, sir,' came the cry from my peers (it seemed I was to be the victim of my own fashionability – not for the first time, nor the last, for that matter).

'No, exactly, because it's a painting of a crude and obnoxious strumpet and it will be removed this instant. Go to the janitor's hut and ask him for some detergent to wash this filth off, and then report to me, you repellent individual.'

I didn't bother visiting the janitor, I simply painted out the offending image and replaced it with 'Grand Funk Railroad' in bold, three-dimensional letters. I had no idea what kind of music Grand Funk Railroad made, but they had a great name and nobody else had heard of them, so that was good enough for me. I wandered around school for the following fortnight telling everybody what GFR sounded like, even though I had never actually heard them.

There was a strange kind of hierarchy that revolved around the thickness of paint on the flap of one's haversack, and with these artistic endeavours I found myself well ahead of boys in years far in advance of mine. And so it continued throughout my school days, until the flap's thickness was in excess of sixteen feet.

*

Luckily, not all the staff at Eastbourne Secondary School were as forbidding as the headmaster. Here are some that I liked.

Miss Ayres was my English teacher. She was rather a large lady who wore flowing, floral kaftans, had a high-stacked blonde beehive hairdo, and drove a Fiat 500 which wasn't much bigger than herself. She must have felt confident with her size, as driving a car that fit her like a shirt and squeezing in and out of it every day in front of hundreds of children would have been quite a strain otherwise. She was a lovely lady though — always chirpy, and very keen on Aesop's fables.

Miss Heaton was my art teacher. She was about 26 years old and quite good-looking, wearing her blonde hair tied back in a pony-tail, with specs and a mini-skirt. The boys were very fond of her. In fact it was not uncommon to see an eager pupil drop his pencil so he could bend down to pick it up as Miss Heaton passed by in the hope of sneaking a peek at her knickers, although this wasn't always necessary.

Once, another boy and I were summoned into the stockroom to assist Miss Heaton with some art materials. She needed to climb a ladder in order to reach these necessary items, and as we stood beneath her, already with a fairly good view, she assisted our scrutiny by cocking her leg out to give us a clear shot of her purple pants. She remained in this position for some time, long enough for us to nudge each other senseless.

This performance may have been accidental, but I'm fairly sure it was for our benefit. Her potentially libidinous nature was further expressed when she announced one day that she was going up to Newcastle to see The Faces in concert at the City Hall, and that with a bit of luck she may wake up tomorrow next to Rod Stewart (being the naive lad that I was, I had to have this comment explained to me by a classmate).

Mr Hodgson also taught English. He was a polio victim and so was in a wheelchair. He always had a copy of the *New Musical Express* on his desk and I would regularly stay back after class to talk to him about music. It may have been coincidence (in fact, it certainly was) but with his longish hair and beard he was a Robert Wyatt look-alike, even though we lived in Wyatt's pre-wheelchair years. It was a sad day when it was announced in assembly that Mr Hodgson had died. I shed a tear knowing that I had lost not only a teacher, but a friend as well.

Doc Thornhill was my maths teacher and must have been at least 90 when he taught us. Rumour had it that he was pensioned off but refused to leave. He always wore a crumpled grey serge suit and was prone to headstands when the urge took him. He had an odd sense of humour that I liked, rather like Will Hay. Come to think of it, he looked like Will Hay as well – maybe he was him.

Doc (he had been a doctor of mathematics at Oxford at some stage) once sent a girl off to the sweetshop to buy him some Everton Mints, and on her return demanded to know where she had been. When she explained that he had sent her himself, he apologised, offered them round the class and told us to eat them in silence while he watched standing on his head.

*

Our house at 59, Hewitson Road was a bow-fronted, semi-detached, 1930s property on the edges of the Eastbourne area of Darlington. Hewitson Road South lay in the Firth Moor area and was a different kettle of fish – it being an estate made up of council houses. And the border you had to cross to enter this estate was Harris Street. Folks north of Harris Street rarely mingled with folks south of Harris Street (which, incidentally, was the birthplace of *Butterflies* star, Wendy Craig).

Entering the Firth Moor estate was a dangerous business if you believed the horror stories. The outskirts weren't too bad – not too dissimilar to our plot really – but as you penetrated the depths of the development, things could get scary. There were areas where grass never grew, neither on pavements nor in front gardens.

How this manifestation of barrenness occurred, I have no idea. Perhaps the parishioners rubbed the grass away with scouring brushes to give the place a more unprepossessing aspect. Or maybe it was a combination of kids rubbing other kids' faces in the dirt and the dogs that travelled around the estate scraping their bottoms along the ground, trying to ease the itching from worms.

In the gardens of many of these houses, collections of unwanted household rubbish were often seen – beds, fridges, children – but one garden in particular stood out. It was the house of 'the dirtiest Hell's Angel in Britain', according to the *Daily Mirror* at the time. His name was Jungle on account of his facial hair, and he lived there with his equally distressed wife. In their front garden, among the various bits of motorcycle and oil cans, old chairs and cider bottles, was a coffin with a swastika painted on the side.

This was Jungle's wife's transport – the sidecar she sat in as Jungle roared around on his blackened Triumph. Everything was black in their world – their clothes, their bikes and their faces – years of oil and grime was caked onto them, giving them an enigmatic chimney-sweep appearance. I would have loved to have seen inside their grubby domicile and marvelled at the sooty interior. Years later I was introduced to Jungle and he turned out to be a thoroughly nice chap.

If entering the Firth Moor estate was like entering Joseph Conrad's *Heart of Darkness*, then Kurtz's compound was the Firth Moor pub: a stark and ugly 1960s drinking chamber, built purely for the purpose of drinking and getting drunk. No frills, no attempt to prettify any area of the building: this was a place where drinking was a serious business and somewhere within those walls was Kurtz, smoking a Woodbine and supping on his pint of keg heavy.

I rarely infiltrated this far, although I did have a friend who lived on the other side of Harris Street, in Hewitson Road South. His name was David Jakeway.

David Jakeway had a Hot Wheels track that was about 30 feet long. It was the latest in toy-car speedways, a kind of MC Escher strip of orange plastic that could be curved and coiled into bends and loops and allow little cars to hurtle down the track at speeds in excess of 2000mph.

We would spend hours in his bedroom setting up the course, manipulating it round pillows and under cupboards and eventually out of the window, sending the cars and their invisible drivers to their deaths as they plunged into the garden below. It was a simple yet superbly effective way of propelling cars at fantastical speeds.

At home I had a Matchbox Motorway, which was prehistoric next to the futuristic Hot Wheels track. I got it for Christmas and by Boxing Day it had seized up beyond repair. This toy was nothing but a cheap version of Scalextric but whereas the vastly superior Scalextric sent cars racing around powered by electricity, the Matchbox Motorway sent Vauxhall Vivas trundling around via a pin on the bottom of the car that was jammed into a long coiled spring that ran the entire length of the road. One kink in the coil and it snarled up, and no amount of trying to straighten it out would cure it.

The first sign of this was a terrible grating sound followed by the smell of burning plastic and culminating in smoke billowing from the transformer before the whole thing died with a horrifying screech. The picture on the box – a Ford Cortina or a Capri tearing down the M1 through the countryside at a thrilling angle – gave a very different vision of the expected excitement lurking within.

And so inevitably I was drawn to David Jakeway's Hot Wheels. He also had other exciting toys, like the Johnny Seven – a huge Tommy gun featuring seven weapons to choose from when in battle with your friends. I could not compete with my puny *The Man From U.N.C.L.E.* pistol against the mighty Johnny Seven with its rocket launcher, rapid-fire ping-pong ball unit, laser beams, water squirter and, for some unknown reason, a thing that seemed to backfire intentionally and shoot coloured balls into your face.

Not only did David have better toys than me, but he also had pubes. These he proudly displayed to me one day, in much the same way as he might reveal a newly acquired bike, or a bound set of Marvel comics.

First he unzipped his trousers, rolled down his underpants and demanded, 'Have you got any of these?' Then promptly – as if to suggest that there were plenty more where they came from – he pulled a cluster out and threw them out of the window. The gossamer-like fleece hung in the air for a moment before being carried away on a summer zephyr in the direction of the railway lines.

I was mildly shocked and replied, without exhibiting, that I too was the owner of a whisper of fur hidden deep in the recesses of my pants. But I certainly wasn't going to unveil them for his perusal, and I was definitely not going to rip out a tuft and lose them forever out of the window.

'You haven't got any, have you?' he taunted,

'Yes, I have,' I lied. 'I've got loads, they're everywhere, it's like a forest. Anyway, my tea's ready now – see ya.' And off I scarpered – home for a full examination in the privacy of my bedroom.

Puberty crept up and struck without my realising. I had noticed that when I climbed up the ropes in the gym during PE lessons I had been experiencing tingling sensations in the groin area. I looked around to see that other boys were also dangling from the top of the ropes – legs kicking like frogs, a look of distracted glee on their gormless faces. It seemed we had begun to mature.

CHAPTER EIGHT

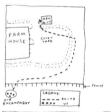

THE HEN HUT

THE FARMER WITH HIS GREASY HAT AND GARMENTS

THE PRIZE

'Birmingham was a big city with loads of churches, and if he was asked which one, Rod had simply to say he couldn't remember'

Girls had begun to appear interesting as opposed to irritating, and I started to look at them with a new curiosity. At junior school, I had had two girlfriends simultaneously – Pauline Robinson and Maureen Cox. Our triangular relationship revolved around me doing drawings for them in art lessons which they would then pass off as their own.

Usually, it seemed, it was a picture of a snarling lion leaping out of the page, and – looking back – I was probably being used. Girls learn early how to manipulate us masculine innocents – in this case by telling me that I did excellent lions and getting me to do their work for them. I didn't mind though, I would bask in the flattery of their honeyed words: 'You're so good at lions, do us another one, quick.' I also got to walk them home, accompanied by cries of, 'Now we know who you go with,' from tormentors who would shadow our whole journey.

The naivety of this alliance was replaced in my first year at secondary school with the early twinkle of lust, and this was directed at a girl called Fiona Hutton. It was her hair that was my chief obsession, a thick mane of strawberry blonde that reached almost down to her waist. I had to get near her, but how?

I was painfully shy when it came to girls. I knew she went to the C of E youth club at St Hilary's but, following enquiries, it appeared you had to be confirmed in order to join. And so I announced – much to Mum and Dad's surprise – that I was ready to take the vows.

Weeks of dull attendance at Bible groups and confirmation classes followed. My constant questioning of miracles and supernatural phenomena in turn raised questions as to whether I was in fact the anti-Christ infiltrating the holiness of these simple lessons. To save myself from being burnt at the stake for heresy, and to secure admittance to the youth club, I kept my mouth shut and did the time.

At last I was welcomed into God's house, and was rewarded with the wine and the biscuit and – most important of all – the membership card to the youth club. It had been a long journey, but I had arrived. I was ready to meet Fiona Hutton and impress her with my witty lines in chat and my faultless style in fashion. This, accompanied by my pop expertise and encyclopaedic knowledge of the Luftwaffe, would have her in the palm of my hand within the week.

The youth club was held in the church hall and boasted a junior pool table as well as a stainless-steel drinks trolley, complete with plastic cups filled with weak Tree Top orange squash and a selection of gypsy creams. The hall was dazzlingly lit with fluorescent strip lights – almost to the point that arc welder's goggles were required. This, presumably, was so Jesus could look down and spot any lascivious behaviour among his children. Even without the watchful eyes of the Messiah on each and every one of us, it was instantly apparent that there was no chance of making a move on a girl under these conditions, and with nothing to do other than watch some kids play pool or stand staring at the drinks trolley, there was no room for showing off. It would have to be an outside job.

Week one was disastrous. On exiting the club I approached Fiona and, with playboy confidence, said, 'That was good, wasn't it?' – as if this dreary experience had been the high point of my week – then turned promptly on my heel and swaggered off into the night.

Week two was slightly better. I blurted out the names of several pop groups as well as a number of World War Two bombers and the precise location of a golden eagle's nest in Tommy Crooks Park. Finishing with a 'see you next week' wink, I swanned off in search of a rifle.

This wasn't working. What I needed was an ally. And so I called on the services of Rod Willcox.

'You must come to the youth club,' I pleaded. 'It's really good fun – there's loads to do.'

He agreed and then I gently dropped in the fact that you had to be confirmed to get in, but not to worry, I had an ingenious plan: he would pretend he had already been confirmed in Birmingham.

This would not be investigated by the vicar, as Birmingham was a big city with loads of churches, and if he was asked which one, Rod had simply to say he couldn't remember. The problem was that Rod had to put on a Brummie accent.

On arrival at the club that week, the plan was executed, but Rod's attempts at Brummie were pitiful. He sounded more Dutch than anything. That, accompanied by the fact that he was far from impressed by the place and had no intention of returning, meant that my move on Fiona had to be now, so I screwed up my courage and asked if I could walk her home that evening.

We strolled away from St Hilary's in silence – me as stiff as a board and she apparently ambivalent. When we reached the back of the Co-op – the place where we were to part – I turned towards her and, as I had seen in the pictures, pushed my face onto hers, holding my breath until I could hold it no more.

On completion of this movement I withdrew and stared at her, awaiting a comment and perhaps marks out of ten. She drew back her head, mouth agape, and for a moment I thought she might vomit, but she didn't; she blew out a bit of air, said, 'See ya,' and walked off.

'See you next week,' I called out, and strolled home with a rolling gait.

The next week, the same thing happened. I pinned her against the wall and rubbed my face on hers for one whole minute (an accurate timing, as this was how long I could stay underwater without breathing), finishing with a confident 'See you next week.'

But it was not to be. The following day at school, Fiona dispatched one of her friends to find me with the devastating news that she didn't want to go out with me any more.

'But why?' I asked.

'Because,' her minion replied, 'you're a rubbish kisser, an' you didn't even try to touch her up.'

The ground opened up into a bottomless chasm as I responded with, 'Well, I thought it polite not to.' That was the precise moment when I gave up on pursuing girls and returned to Airfix models and records. Well, for the time being, anyway.

*

At this stage, after-school activities still revolved chiefly around the theft of birds' eggs and general rural mischief. But Steve Hodgson and I were about to embark on an evening pursuit that would raise scientific research to a new pitch of intensity. A new Hinton's supermarket had been built on Yarm Road at the top of Hewitson Road, and around the back of it was a large area of waste ground where an old factory used to be (this would also be the site of our amphibian-collecting forays, but more of that later).

Tools were discarded and strewn about once the Hinton's was completed, presumably dropped by the builders where they stood when the whistle was blown signifying the completion of the project as they sped towards the Wheatsheaf pub. Anyway, Steve and I put them to good use by digging two graves in the middle of the wasteland and feathering them with grasses, rags and any soft material, in much the same way a chaffinch might furnish her nest. The next step was to lie down in our respective trenches and wait for nightfall so we could begin our work.

Our task was to dissect the universe – from the smallest sub-atomic particle to the largest and farthest star – and form theories on how it all worked; how space and time never began, nor would ever end; how this related to theology; how our solar system started; and, more importantly, how it could be destroyed with the massive anti-matter electron weapon we had been developing in Steve's bedroom. More important even than that was what would happen to us once we had destroyed the solar system.

The answer was simple. Due to the magnetic pull from the outer edges of time and space, we would expand into astronomically colossal brains that would control everything around us. But if we consumed our own universe, then who would we control? The next universe of course. And the one beyond that, and the one beyond that … to infinity.

But then we would be back to being tiny insignificant brains, floating about with no home or friends or Mum and Dad, for ever and ever, because time never ends. As we expanded, we would also probably become immortal, but since we were just floating brains with no mouths, we wouldn't be able to complain or shout for help. And even if we could, no one would be there to hear us.

What a mess we had created. We emerged from our craters, our minds aching with the turmoil of it, and headed off home to revise the schedule of mass destruction.

On the same site as our evening space-pits, we would spend the day exploring the various ponds, looking for creatures like great diving beetles, pond-skaters, whirlygig beetles, frogs, toads and newts – the greatest prize being the great crested newt: the biggest and most dinosaur-like of the amphibians, and a real rarity. These animals and insects would be caught by hand, transferred into a large pickling jar filled with pond water and taken home and relocated into a large galvanised bathtub that I had seated on top of the coal bunker.

It was well designed, with the aim of giving the pond creatures every comfort, with weeds and rocks and hidey holes. I would sit staring into the tub for hours studying the behaviour of the beasts and, on the introduction of a new species into the environment, watch and see how it reacted with its neighbours. The hope always was that the new introduction may do battle with one of the other creatures in a spectacular clash-of-the-titans-style engagement, but this never happened. Although bloody duels between great diving beetles and great crested newts were occasionally reported at school, there was never any hard evidence and these stories were usually put about by kids who wanted to be a part of the in-crowd.

One of these desperate individuals used to watch us at our pond work and try and befriend us with periodic cries and calls from behind bushes and walls. We ignored him but he persisted and slowly he encroached on our territory and began to fish about in nearby ponds, muttering to himself, 'Mumble, mumble, salamander, mumble, massive specimen, mumble, unidentified new species'. We knew there was something not right about this impostor and decided to move on to ponds new and leave him to our well-scoured area – he could have it.

Two weeks later we returned to the site around the back of Hinton's and the weird kid was still there.

'Over here,' he shouted. 'Come and see what I've got – you'll love it.'

Intrigued, we cautiously approached.

He stood there, seeming very pleased with himself, and asked, 'What do you think?'

We looked about and couldn't see anything. 'What?' we enquired.

'There,' he said with apparently abounding self-satisfaction, and then we saw it. Behind him was a hawthorn tree covered in newts that he had pinned to the thorns and allowed to perish, like hundreds of amphibious criminals lynched and displayed as a warning to others.

'What do you think?' he grinned. Struck dumb by this horrific spectacle, we left him to his callous task, resolving to give him a wide berth in future. The sad part of it is, I now realise that his vile act was probably intended to gain our approval.

*

I had little or no interest in sport at this time. Football was anathema, and my lack of feeling for the game was all too apparent in my attempts to play it. Like Casper in Ken Loach's *Kes*, I was always the last to be picked for a side, and would then be dispatched to the goal area, where I swung from the posts, or stood with my hands down my shorts looking at the sky.

According to the school rules, I was forced to engage in at least one team sport, so I plumped for rugby. And I became rather good at it. It was agreed by Mr Carling and Mr Mason, the sports masters, that I should be best placed in the scrum as a prop, even though I was about the same weight and frame as a young Russian gymnast. I may have been slight, but I had speed and could dispatch the ball with some swiftness up the wing, so long as no brutish boys tried to stop me. But brutish boys trying to stop me was the name of the game, and this was where I revealed my secret skills.

I would speed up the wing until an opponent headed towards me, then I dropped my jaw, giving myself a slack-mouthed appearance (a bit of slaver dripping down the side of the mouth was a bonus). I would then roll my eyes upwards, sideways and wherever I could persuade them to wander and let out a low moan, giving myself the demeanour of an escaped mental patient. This manoeuvre (as previously outlined in Chapter 1) would unsettle my rival and thus allow me the chance to side-step them and avoid a clash.

My faux mental-patient ruse was so successful that I was recruited onto the school team and briefly became a star player. Unfortunately, this meant playing games on a Saturday morning and that was something I really didn't want to do as it interfered with proper work like egg and newt collection, Airfix modelling and walking-stick microphone technique practice.

Many a morning Dad had to prise me away from a pot of Humbrol paint and a Fiesler Storch model plane and load me grumbling into the car to employ my special techniques on the sports field. But this annoyance would be transferred into my performance on the pitch, and my faces would become even more grotesque in the heat of battle. My tongue would loll and curl from my mouth and my lower jaw would jut out, baring my bottom teeth – this, alongside the squints and a new develop-ment in the shape of twitching and violent jerks, making me an even more frightening opponent.

Another distraction I employed was the wearing of scarlet shorts, as opposed to the rest of the team's white ones. I don't know how I got away with this, but I did for the entire three years of my rugby career. It all came to an end one frosty morning when we played Haughton School – notoriously vicious and underhand in their tactics – and my facial contortions were mocked and passed off as pathetic theatrics (which, indeed, was exactly what they were).

One of these savage brutes grabbed me by the plums and lifted me from the ground, spun me 360 degrees in the air, and hurled me off the pitch into a frozen puddle. This was the first time my young nuts had experienced such savagery and the shock sent waves of nausea shuddering through my frame until I deposited my sugar puffs onto the icy ground. With watery eyes, I hobbled off to the changing rooms vowing never to play again.

Shortly after this attack, my friend Brian Mitchell was heard howling following another barbaric assault by one of the Haughtonians. He too was escorted back to the changing rooms, this time with a broken arm.

We sat whimpering in the back of Dad's Renault as he drove us to the Memorial Hospital, where Brian got his arm plastered and I had my balls poked by an ancient, bearded physician. And that was the last time I displayed my extraordinary skills on the rugby field.

Team sports never really held much appeal for me, but I found more to enjoy in the solo variety. In fact, in 1970 I was the fastest boy in the county at the hundred-yard dash held at Featham's football ground. I held this record for a whole half an hour, until a boy named 'Rocket' took it away from me with a blistering display of gazelle-like speed. I was also reasonably adept at leaping long distances into sand in the long jump. This was presumably a skill developed in the course of long hours spent 'beck jumping' – a rural game of springing over streams.

However, it was water sports that I loved the most. Swimming was a big deal in our family. We were always in the water somewhere – in the sea, in rivers, in freezing mountain streams or in the Gladstone swimming baths. In fact, Dad built one of the first surfboards in the region some time in the late 1960s. It was a three-foot disc of plywood with a blue and red lightning-strike motif in the middle, and we would ride the waves at Redcar like it was Malibu.

I took all my swimming exams with enthusiasm and got the lot instantly – proudly displaying the badges on the lapel of my school blazer, alongside my cycling proficiency badge and Tufty Club button, broadcasting the news that not only could I swim and ride a bike, but I was talented at crossing roads as well.

Whenever the opportunity arose I would immerse myself. Evenings were spent in the River Tees at Blackwell or Coniscliffe, thrashing about in the brown peaty waters – turning somersaults far beneath the surface until I had no idea which way was up and only gravity saved me from a watery grave. At Coniscliffe – or 'Conny' as we called it – there was a rope attached to a tree which enabled the stout of heart to swing out over the water. By all accounts there was also a submerged spike that would spear you should you land in the wrong place, but that didn't stop us.

At Blackwell there was a 'mudbath' – a hollow in the river-bank that would fill with mud, given enough encouragement from river water and flailing youths. Once this aperture was filled with glorious gloop, we would roll about in it until completely covered in the thick sludge, and then slide down a mud-chute into the river where we would be cleansed of our filth, ready for a repeat performance.

We were washing away the clay during one of these mud-festivals when I noticed an oily rainbow-coloured slime drifting by, followed by a rich and pungent odour. Gazing upstream in search of the source of the slick, I saw a group of Hell's Angels bathing, fully clad, in the river a short distance away.

They were frolicking like young children – splashing one another, their iron crosses glinting in the hot sun. Helmets were being used to collect water to toss at their companions in a carefree manner. They were such a lovely sight as they tossed their heads from side to side in rapturous joy, beads of silvery water cascading from their beards and the once blackened, oily visages slowly revealing the rosy cherubic faces beneath. One of the creatures turned in my direction and as our eyes met, he offered a benign smile, to which I answered with a wave. We were united in our aquatic element.

CHAPTER NINE

'We didn't want to be smoothies anyway, and had no interest in aggro, nor throwing bricks at passing effluent'

Brian Mitchell lived on Harris Street, and we walked to school together every day. I was always slightly in awe of Brian. He had deep red hair that appeared to grow about six inches a week, a brother who was a teddy boy, and platform boots that had two-inch soles.

These impressed me very much. I adored footwear, and would often dream of shoes and boots. In fact, one Sunday morning I took a bus all the way to Stockton, just to look at a pair of high-leg moccasin-fringed suede boots that someone had told me about. Even though the shop was shut, I stood in front of the window, drinking in the wonder of the boot.

Rod Willcox's dad wore a pair of twin-zipped Chelsea boots that I was obsessed with, so much so that I would contrive ways of getting low enough down in his presence so as to give them a close inspection. I once got to handle them when he had removed them and was slumbering in his chair. How I marvelled at the dual zip action, and the simple fact that each boot had two zips for no reason whatsoever. They were a purplish-red colour with paper-thin soles and just a nod towards a Cuban heel. Lovely.

I owned a pair of brown platform slip-on loafers. These were covered in a special kind of plastic coating that peeled off in chunks almost immediately after purchase. They also had one-inch soles which would lead to regular ankle injuries as I attempted to control their passage along the streets. Such injuries were commonplace amongst the platform-wearing children at school, eventually leading to the banning of this type of footwear – somewhat after the fact, as they were already drifting out of fashion by the time of the ruling.

Anyway, more of shoes later. One day, as Brian Mitchell and I were hobbling to school together, he suggested that we should have a secret sign that only we two would recognise and use it as a form of greeting – a kind of early version of the 'crips' and 'bloods' hand signals. He offered up something that I had amazingly never seen before – the two-fingered salute, the old English bowmen's offering to the French, the inverted victory V, proffered twice at the receiver.

How I had never noticed this controversial gesture being used prior to this moment I don't know, but I hadn't, and thought it the perfect secret sign. Brian must have grasped my innocence eagerly and encouraged me to give the salute to passing motorists and busloads of people on our way to and from school, telling me that none of them had a clue what it meant.

Arriving home with Brian that afternoon, I approached Mum, Dad and Lois, who were already sitting at the dinner table, asked them if Brian could stay for tea, and gave them all the new secret sign, with a cocky, knowing smile on my face. Dad erupted from the table demanding an explanation for this outrageous insult.

'It's me and Brian's secret symbol,' I explained, curious to know how they knew it, and worried that it had caused so much consternation. Dad sat me down and explained that it was a well-known offensive gesture and well I knew it, and don't think we didn't know that I knew it. I didn't know it before, but I did then, and looking over at Brian, I knew he knew it as well. I had been duped. Brian was sent home and on his way out I suggested that we modify the salute in favour of a single finger in the middle of the hand. He walked away shaking his head in despair.

Secret signs and societies were a vital part of life, and two of my classmates – Johnny Thubron and Stuey Ward – were members of a group known as SPAM, or Skerne Park Aggro-Men. Out of school they wore Doc Martens, riding boots or brogues, Sta-Prest trousers and Ben Sherman shirts in the style of latter-day skinheads but with longer crops – a style which identified them as 'Smoothies'. Myself and Brian Mitchell enquired as to how we might join SPAM, and were told that there was a gruelling initiation ceremony that we would have to go through if we were to become members, and we should call round at Stuey's house that evening, ready to face this ordeal.

We arrived promptly and were met by Stuey and Johnny and taken outside to a square green surrounded by houses where the test was to take place. 'OK,' said Stuey, 'this is what you have to do. The first part is that you have to run around the green in less than one minute.' This we did with flying colours. We were halfway to becoming Aggro-Men, although the prospect was looking less appealing by the minute.

The second and final part of the initiation required us to get into the drains. We trooped off into the fields around the back of the estate and were led to a manhole cover on a concrete slab, whereupon Johnny and Stuey lifted the cover to reveal a ladder leading down into a dark and smelly underground chamber. We descended into the fetid gloom and found ourselves in a room twenty feet by ten with a sewage stream running through it.

'Now,' announced Johnny, 'you have to take three bricks and throw them at the turds as they float by. When you hit one you have to shout "Bismarck!" We'll take score – and you have to hit all three.'

This we did with equal success and emerged triumphant from the noxious chamber, theoretically ready to have our member-ship accepted, although by this stage we had changed our minds – we didn't want to be Smoothies anyway, and had no interest in aggro, nor throwing bricks at passing effluent – so we thanked them for their indulgence, and walked homeward, making plans for our own gang – an assemblage of flamboyant glam-rockers known as 'The Boys' – which seemed a project much more fitting to our temperaments.

'The Boys' was a relatively short-lived gang phenomenon. Our sense of collective identity was established by wearing brogues with soles completely covered in hob-nails, which we called segs, or blakeys as they were sometimes called, and painted in fluores-cent colours.

This enabled your feet to glow iridescently as you cycled past your friends, feet spinning in the pedals. You could then send showers of sparks into the night air by thrusting the metal studs down onto the Tarmac as you sped by – thereby creating a kind of home-made light show emanating from the feet. My brogues were painted a luminous red which caused great excitement amongst my peers, and great disappointment to Mum when she saw what I had done to my school shoes.

*

As school sports were, by this time, an activity that I was not in any way partial to, I was pleased to learn that I had the option of choosing to work in the community instead. This meant being dispatched to a pensioner's house to do good works with their gardens, clean their properties, paint the woodwork or perform some such simple service.

Brian Mitchell and myself were sent to visit an old lady called Edith, who must have been at least an octogenarian. She lived alone in a semi-detached house on McMullen Road, on the outskirts of town.

The house was typical for a lady of her years – quite Victorian in appearance, with lace doilies, heavy mahogany furniture and the smell of meat pies and wood polish hanging heavy and dense in the air like a warm fog. In the front room was a piano that had been sitting in the same position since she and her late husband moved into the house in the 1930s, when – I guess – the houses were built.

As I noodled around on the piano, I noticed that there was a bullet lodged in between two keys, two-thirds of the way up the keyboard. My mind erupted with a thousand fanciful explanations. Had she shot her husband after years of intolerable performances on the piano? Had our predecessors been cruelly disposed of as they polished the instrument, and later turned into meat pies? Or was she a spy who was regularly visited by snipers wishing to snuff her out?

The answer was none of these, she explained, pointing at a hole in the window where the bullet had made its entrance – it was now sealed with a piece of Sellotape, but it was still clearly visible. The story was that during the Second World War a stricken Lancaster was limping home from a bombing raid, trying to get to nearby Middleton Airfield (now Teesside Airport, which has in turn, recently been renamed the much more catchy 'South Durham Tees Valley but not quite in Teesside Airport').

The pilot, a Canadian named McMullen, had ordered his crew to bale out – leaving him the valiant task of flying the crippled aircraft over the town and not crashing it onto civilian homes. This he did, and the doomed bomber and its pilot were destroyed in the fields next to Edith's home. As the plane exploded, the rear gun involuntarily fired off a round of bullets and one of them went straight through her front window and lodged itself in the piano, where it remained to that day. McMullen became a war hero, the name of the road was changed to McMullen Road in his honour, and the bullet lay there as testament to his bravery.

Edith was a lively and cheerful old lady and the first task we were given by her was to go down to the local bakery and fetch her some cinnamon buns and a bottle of Lowcock's lemonade. On returning we found she had laid the small table in her parlour with a crisp white macramé tablecloth and three china plates and beakers.

The three of us sat and ate the cakes and drank the lemonade together, and then she produced a pack of playing cards, asking what our favourite games might be. I was pretty good at gin rummy and proudly made this claim, only to be scoffed at for favouring an 'old lady's game'.

Edith said she would teach us poker instead, enquiring as she did as to how much money we had on us. We admitted – much to her disappointment – that we were penniless, but she agreed to accept IOUs should she win. And win she did. Every game we were roundly trounced and a pile of IOUs mounted on the table amongst the cinnamon crumbs. The following week, the same thing happened – this time accompanied by the offer of a small drop of whisky in our lemonade, and a George Formby film playing on the TV in the background.

Back at school, we heard tales from our fellow community workers of cruel masters who forced them to dig trenches in the garden or tidy decades' worth of rotting rubbish in the garage until their spirits were quite fragmented by these aged overlords. We, on the other hand, boasted of our easy-going mistress, with whom we gambled, ate and boozed the afternoons away whilst watching TV. Not only this, but she would let us go home whenever we wanted.

We should have kept our mouths shut, because some jealous grass reported us, and when we returned to Edith's house, she told us she had had a visit from a supervisor and she should now put us to work digging her borders or some such menial task. She had a plan, though. We would do a bit of digging and leave the tools out as if we were working in case anyone should call round to check. This they duly did and we leapt into position accordingly, dousing ourselves with dabs of lemonade to look sweaty and huffing and puffing in the most dramatic and hammy way.

Edith died a couple of years later. She didn't want anybody to dig her garden. She just wanted some company – someone to listen to her stories, and a pair of unsophisticated gambling partners with whom to have a flutter. And we were more than happy to fill that vacancy.

*

The fields and woods that stretched away from McMullen Road were my territory. I spent an unnatural amount of time there – making dens, destroying ants' nests, igniting gorse bushes etc. There was an old farm there, owned by a farmer and his two sons who could quite easily have emerged from some distant swamp in Louisiana. This family's coarse ways and hillbilly demeanour came to the fore one day, as we innocently occupied ourselves by stealing eggs from their henhouse.

Myself, Steve Hodgson, Alan Ianson and a new mystery kid sat by the perimeter fence dressed entirely in combat gear – or as near to it as we could muster, e.g. wellie boots worn over jeans and anoraks, with hoods pulled tight around the face so only eyes and noses were visible. We rounded these outfits off with a fair amount of mud plastered onto salient areas of skin – giving us the appearance of a crack team of birdwatchers, engaged in secret operations deep in the equatorial jungle.

Our plan was as follows. One by one we were going to creep, flat on our bellies, around the outer areas of the farm, then sprint across the courtyard into the henhouse, fill our pockets with as many eggs as possible, and return to base to have our eggs counted. The man returning with the most eggs was the victor, and would be hailed thus for ever more.

The first infantryman to crawl his way round to the chickens was Alan. We watched as he slid carefully along, our eyes twitching betwixt him and the farmhouse, ready to give the secret call should anyone appear at a window. The cry was, as usual with any business like this, a kind of kookaburra crossed with a dying

Cyclops, which would blend in seamlessly with the wood pigeons and sheep that provided the rest of the ambience.

Alan returned with a magnificent collection of seven whole eggs, and six more crushed in the breast pocket of his anorak. Next up was Hodgy. We slapped him on the back and wished him luck on this most perilous of journeys. He scuttled off on his mission like a crab out of a bucket, and returned from the henhouse with nine eggs. I was up next, and had to come back with at least ten to be in the running for the title of 'Egg Lord'.

Off I went, employing a kind of rolling movement, followed by a caterpillar wriggle. It was important to present a suitably impressive style of movement for future reference when relating these daring deeds to friends. Halfway round the farmyard I saw movement. It was the farmer, and I hoped to God that no one else saw him and delivered the warning call, or the game would be up.

He stood there for what seemed like an age, with his oily coat, greasy cap and buttery trousers held together with bits of rope and twine. I lay there trembling and nearly sick with fear, then, with a violent cough and an odd arm jerk, he fiddled about with his trousers and began to urinate on his dog, which immediately scurried off back indoors.

When he followed, I breathed a sigh of relief and carried on with my journey. I reached the henhouse and entered, beady chicken eyes penetrating the very core of my being. I was there to steal their produce and this I did; filling my pockets with the warm eggs and placing a final one in my mouth – the emulsifying taste of calcium, straw and chicken shit merging with my saliva.

Nervously I returned to my comrades and displayed my pitiful bounty. Only three eggs had survived – two in my sweaty hands and the one in my mouth – the rest had been crushed in my pockets in my urgency to retreat back to base. I was the least successful egg thief, although I took the prize (at least in my own mind) for that unusual creeping technique and my patented mouth transportation method.

Finally, it was the turn of the mysterious kid (who had joined our party at the last minute, and whom we only vaguely knew). He successfully reached the chickens, but whatever he did in the hut made them start squawking and honking in a most clamorous manner – causing the farmer's sons to come running from the house to investigate. He was dragged, screaming, from the henhouse and pulled violently to and fro by the two hillbillies as they interrogated him.

As they bundled him into the back of their van and drove off out of the yard, it was clear that our daring commando unit had lost its newest recruit. The last we saw of him was his frightened face peering out of the back window, his hands banging on the glass as he bewailed his lost freedom.

We found him later – wandering, slightly dazed, around the fields, red-eyed and mumbling. Apparently the farmer's sons had not been particularly concerned with the fact that he'd been caught trespassing and stealing eggs, but were more interested to find out if he had any dirty magazines on him, and – more oddly – whether he had discovered the hiding places of their stash of pornography, which they had forgotten about in much the same way that squirrels forget the hiding places of their winter nut supply.

Our mystery member had told them he had neither men's magazines nor information regarding their forgotten cache, but they hadn't believed him and drove him to a barn where he was tied to a timber post and horsewhipped until he divulged the details they so desperately required. When they were satisfied that he knew nothing, our co-conspirator was released with a warning that if he, or any of his friends, discovered any of the lost mucky mags and didn't report to them, they would be hunted down and shot.

That was the last time we did the poultry run, although months later I discovered an old log in the woods stuffed with cheap top-shelf publications, presumably one of the amnesiac farmer's boys' misplaced hoards.

*

To me, as a teenager, living on the border of town and country was the best of both worlds. I loved the countryside – the woods, the moors, the wildlife, and the balance of chaos and system therein. But I also loved the town – the history that created it, its people, and the shops that sold me my clothes, records and books.

Various money-making schemes were employed to earn the funds to buy these latter necessities. One of the most successful of these ideas was painting schoolmates' haversacks. I already had one of the thickest paint-layered bags in school, and it regularly featured a new and brilliant piece of artwork – much admired by kids with lesser artistic skills who wanted to appear at the cutting edge of playground fashion.

This was something of a catch-22 situation for the cooler kids. To have a naked, unpainted haversack was the epitome of nerdi-ness – only the lonely went about with a nude bag. But what if you were a 'tough' or a 'cat', yet had no artistic skills? You would be mocked by your peers and giggled at behind your back by younger, uncool kids as they looked sideways at your crude attempts at the face of Newcastle United's Malcolm McDonald – a.k.a. 'SuperMac' – which ended up looking more like Galen from *Planet of the Apes*.

This was therefore an opening for me, and I could charge whatever I wanted within reason as there was no competition, so I did. It was 50p for a quick job, £1 for a reasonable picture, and £2 for the full works. I would also do a bit of customising to give their haversacks the 'long drop' look. This meant that the straps of the bag were buckled together so it hung extra low over the shoulder. For an even longer drop, an extra strap could be added so the bag hung just above ground level.

Another scheme was gathering bulrushes from the disused quarry round the back of school and selling bunches of them door to door. Hodgy and I came up with this plan whilst fishing for newts one day, and spent the morning wading around gathering the rushes, which we then separated into bunches of ten and sold to housewives for 20p a bunch. We later heard through the grapevine that these bulrushes had quickly begun to fester and emit vile stenches, as well as harbouring a selection of bloodsucking swamp insects, so we left that scheme alone in future.

The quarry was an exciting place to indulge fantasies in. It could look like a set from *Star Trek* or *Doctor Who* or, from another angle, a scene from *The Seventh Voyage of Sinbad*. It was perfect for swimming, hide-and-seek, mudslides and 'shitty-shotty', which was hoying 'clemmies' off the end of a stick, a.k.a. throwing small compacted balls of mud from the end of a three-foot rod and seeing how far you could make them travel.

The advent of black dustbin bags caused this game to develop in a more dangerous direction. A fire would be lit at night and a bin bag was wound around the end of the stick. This was then plunged into the blaze until the bag had melted onto the end of it. Once removed from the fire, the burning projectile was hurled into the night sky like an incendiary bomb.

This all went wrong on one occasion when I tossed one of these flaming plastic balls through the air and it landed squarely on Hodgy's face. His howls reverberated around the quarry, sending roosting widgeons into a panic and causing them to flee their night-time lodgings. The plastic cooled swiftly, adhering to Hodgy's face in a manner that seemed irreversible. The following day he appeared at school looking like a black Phantom of the Opera, with glossy plastic scabs glued to his face which we were invited to gently peel off and keep as souvenirs.

A few weeks later, it was my turn to take it on the face when Hodgy and I went for an evening cycle ride that took us further than we had anticipated. As darkness fell, we had travelled eight miles from home and began to descend a steep hill at speed. I hit a stone and went hurtling over the handlebars – my face heading straight for the Tarmac. I could hear Hodgy cackling as he witnessed my misfortune, but his laughter quickly ceased when he too ran into some dark obstacle and went flying as well.

We plunged down the hill, tumbling and sliding until we reached the bottom, our bikes following and crashing into us as we lay moaning in the twilight, torn clothes and bodies in a twisted heap. Fortunately, we had come to rest outside a petrol station, and we went into the toilets to get cleaned up. My face was a mess. The right side had been skinned and was filled with pieces of gravel. It seemed as if I had slid down the road using my face as a brake.

Hodgy appeared uninjured, but then began to complain of pains in his shoulder. I poked it and he screamed. Something wasn't right. The attendant came in to see what was happening and after a quick medical examination declared that it was probably a broken collarbone.

A driver who had stopped for petrol offered to take Hodgy home or to the hospital in his truck, whereas I would be fine riding back alone. Off they went, and I began my long ride home with my ripped garments and ragged face – the trip being made worse by the fact that it began to rain, and then to pelt down in a manner which felt like needles piercing my naked flesh.

I began to chant along with the pushes on the pedals – 'Gotta get home, Gotta get home, Gotta get home' – all the time, the rain stabbing me to the point of nausea. Eventually I reached my own front door looking like the veteran of some terrible battle, and tried to act nonchalant in front of Mum.

'Oh my God!' she cried. 'What happened?'

'What?' I replied. 'I just went out for a bike ride, and fell off … a bit.' The next morning my wound had begun to scab over. Over the course of the following days the scab grew thicker and darker, and I generously offered friends the opportunity to pick bits off as souvenirs. To my surprise, there were no takers.

CHAPTER
TEN

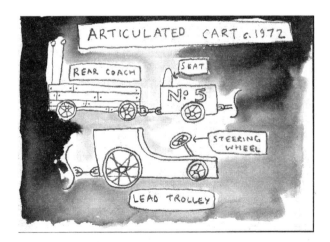

ARTICULATED CART c. 1972

REAR COACH

SEAT

No. 5

STEERING WHEEL

LEAD TROLLEY

'I could have a space-bird!'

The summer holidays of '72 were a memorable time for a number of reasons, one of them being that I had begun seeing my first proper girlfriend. This debut romance was with a Catholic girl named Theresa, who lived with her parents and twelve brothers and sisters in a three-bedroom house. She lived just up the road from my friend Stuart Hutchins, and we met when she came over to investigate what on earth we were doing on the pavement with old pram wheels, springs, bits of wood and rope.

'It's going to be an articulated cart when it's finished,' I told her. She nodded, apparently uninterested, and walked off – offering me a smile as she turned, and not a patronising one either. There was something in that smile that gave me unnatural stirrings in the small of my back.

'I think she likes you,' said Stuart. 'But watch out – she's fourteen.' To a thirteen-year-old boy, a fourteen-year-old girl is an immense chasm of intellect, sophistication, maturity and dreaded sexuality. She was cool all right – she had displayed that – but there was something else about her that I couldn't quite put my finger on.

And then it was pointed out to me by Stuart that she had no eyebrows, nor eyelashes. She did, though, have long shiny brown hair on the top of her head. The lack of eye-hair made her infinitely fascinating to me. She had the look of somebody other-worldly – an alien. I could be going out with a girl from another planet, I could have a space-bird!

Over the succeeding days, our contact became more regular. She would come over and check the progress of our cart and we would go for short strolls chatting about T-Rex, and how satin loon pants were the way forward and would probably never go out of fashion – not in our lifetimes anyway. After a week of strolls, I decided to ask her a question. My stomach performed several revolutions and my voice rose a couple of octaves as I halt-ingly enquired, 'Are we going out with each other?'

'If you want to,' came her welcome reply.

'Yes, I do … please,' I said, getting that feeling again – like mice scurrying up and down my spine and taking occasional trips around the front as well. And with that settled, I put my arms around her, held my breath and nutted her.

'Not like that,' she observed, rubbing her bruised face with her hand. She then gave me a demonstration of how adult-to-adult kissing should be undertaken, and that was it; a kissing frenzy began. We timed our kisses, hoping to become entries in the *Guinness Book of Records* (the record being twelve minutes). We performed upside-down kisses, and – most daringly – the kind of kisses where tongues met.

We were well enough acquainted now for me to enquire as to

whether she really was an alien and why she had no eyebrows. The answer was that she had fallen from a tree when she was young and all her hair had fallen out. It grew back on her head, but nowhere else – she was hairless from the pole down.

Some days were spent at Theresa's friend's house – a tall girl named Pam, who giggled constantly and would do things like shinning up the drainpipe when she knew you were on the toilet and shrieking through the window, or draping herself semi-dressed around the curtains and collapsing to the floor, ripping the drapes from their hooks and laughing like a maniac.

Pam had a brother who was even more demented than she. He was my age but had a haircut that looked like it had been eaten, and a home-made tattoo that appeared to read 'elvis', although it could easily have been 'helvish' as it was boxed in a kind of ladder design. I didn't enquire due to lack of interest. He, like his sister, had a penchant for surprising actions, and one day he offered us the opportunity to watch him eat a sandwich. This seemed an unusually dull offer until he revealed the contents of his two slices of bread. Within them were two terrapins, fresh from his small fish tank, and one of them was bitten in half.

We decided it was time to stop visiting Pam and her clearly deranged brother, but he had one final request – that he might accompany me and Stuart and some other friends on a fishing trip the next day. Given his passion for eating live aquatic creatures, we thought it might be an amusing farewell.

We sat on the banks of the Tees at Middleton One Row with our rods, dangling maggots into the water – the idiot brother giving demonstrations of how many maggots could be stored in the mouth at one time, and generally digging around muttering to himself. We had brought along some food – baked beans, sausages and bread – and pots and pans to cook them in, along with any fish we might catch.

When it was time for lunch, I went to get the cooking gear, but the pot had vanished. 'Has anyone seen the pot?' I enquired. 'It was here with the rest of the stuff, but now it's gone.'

'I've seen it,' said the moronic sibling.

'Well, where is it?' I asked.

'There,' he replied, pointing out into the middle of the river. The cooking pot was drifting by with steam rising from within it.

'What's it doing out there, and what's that steam coming out of it?' I demanded.

'Oh,' he laughed in his unhinged way. 'I took it upstream and had a poo in it, and then set it free on the river.'

We went home and left him there – feverishly stabbing at a tree with his shoe – and never saw nor heard of him again.

*

My romance with Theresa continued unabated, and eventually she awarded me a token of her love, in the form of a lovebite to the neck. The kissing lark had gone too far.

'What did you do that for?' I screamed.

'It means you belong to me,' came the answer.

I spent the next few sweltering summer days wearing a polo-necked jumper to hide the ugly blemish. Dad knew exactly what had happened and let me suffer in the intolerable heat until one day he asked, 'Has it gone yet?'

'What?'

'Your hickey – your lovebite,' he giggled.

Oh, what a fool I had been, thinking I could deceive my parents by wearing rollnecks and fancy scarves in the heat of summer, but how much greater had been my foolishness in allowing a girl to inflict such a monstrous blotch on me in the first place?

It was time, I thought, to cool it with Theresa and concentrate on completing the articulated cart. We moved the construction site to my house, away from Theresa and her ever-pursed lips, lips whose touch I still lusted after, but knew I must deny myself.

In the final week of the holidays, we finished the cart. It had three sections to it, and was about half the size of a normal go-cart, but that made it even more extraordinary. People gathered round and admired the craftsmanship and design and we took it off for a test run in the car park of Cummins' factory.

All was going well, until a gaggle of big lads came over the horizon, all of whom looked intent on spoiling our fun. This was exactly what they proceeded to do – crushing the rear two coaches with their bovver boots, and then riding away on the front chariot, grunting like apes.

Given the seemingly traumatic nature of this episode, we were surprisingly unbothered by it. Perhaps it was the fact that we had at least managed to complete our task and bask in the momentary glory. Perhaps it was simply weariness at the end of the long, drawn-out construction process. Either way, we went home and prepared to return to school for our third year.

There was, however, one final summer holiday celebration still to come: a party at someone's house near school. Everyone would be there and so off I went. I looked and felt very groovy with my hair chopped and sticking up like a cockatoo's, and my pale blue, scoop-necked T-shirt and split-knee loons.

Then a girl came up to me and said, 'You go out with Theresa, don't you?'

'Well,' I replied, 'I ... er ... I don't really ... er ...'

'Well,' she continued, 'she's upstairs on the bed, and she wants to see you.'

'OK,' I gulped, and strolled slowly towards the stairs. Then I turned right out of the front door and legged it home as if being chased by the devil himself.

CHAPTER ELEVEN

'The soup, it transpired, was made from the pigs' testicles we had removed'

My most important educational experiences of the following autumn were to take place outside the sombre confines of Eastbourne Secondary.

A new shop had opened at the top of the street. Where the sweet shop used to be was now an off-licence. This was of no interest to me, unless I required a bottle of Lowcock's or a Tizer . However, one warm afternoon, as I cycled along McMullen Road, I was beckoned over into the fields where a gang of vague school-friends were sitting sipping on cans of beer.

'Here, have a tin,' said one of the slightly tipsy youths.

'Where did you get these?' I enquired.

'We nicked them from behind the new off-licence, they've just moved in and they've left all their stock outside in the yard, so we helped ourselves.'

Two crimes for the price of one: underage drinking and theft – contraband liquor, pilfered plonk, embezzled booze. I was deep within a criminal fraternity. I was on a slippery slope. The feds could arrive at any time and I would be caught up in this crookedness and whisked away to a young offenders' prison.

'Go on then, give us a tin,' I said boldly, and took a long draught of the illicit hooch. It was revolting, although I didn't let it show. My face remained cool and collected, although inside I was wincing at the taste of the disgusting brew.

'Yeah,' I confirmed, 'that's good beer – it's quite malty.' I had heard Dad opine that a particular beer was 'quite malty', so it seemed the right kind of thing to say, and having nothing much else to contribute, I expanded upon this theme.

'In fact, it's very malty. It's probably the maltiest beer I've ever had. And I've had some malty beers in my time, but in the end this is maybe a bit too malty for even my tastes, so I'll leave it if you don't mind, and go home …' and off I cycled. I felt I had got out of that one rather successfully, even if I did feel a bit squiffy and light-headed, so much so that as I wove my way home, I rammed my front wheel into the kerb and bent the front forks.

This was a disaster. What would I tell Mum and Dad? This was my new bike, the one that Dad had spent weeks building from bits of top-quality racing bikes in the garage, and now it was buckled beyond repair. I couldn't tell them the truth; I had to concoct a believable yarn that would get me off the hook. Perhaps I could say that a powerful gust of wind blew the bike against a wall, or that I plummeted into a sinkhole, or a fissure that mysteriously opened up before me.

When I finally arrived home, I went for the safest bet.

'I was riding along McMullen Road when a puppy ran out in front of me and I skidded to avoid it and ran into a tree,' I blurted. Then I made the fatal error of trying to hedge my bets. 'I think it was a puppy, it might have been a pigeon – it all happened so quickly.' Whether I was believed or not, I couldn't be certain, but

I did know that knock-off booze was a bad deal and I vowed to avoid it in the future.

Drink and drugs were unheard of as a recreation at school, at least amongst the kids. Rumours were occasionally heard of gin-soaked teachers being discovered sleeping in stock cupboards, but I never came across any of my peers imbibing anything inside the school gates. Although there was one kid who told me that the way to achieve maximum enjoyment from listening to Hawkwind's In Search of Space album was to smoke dried banana skins or, failing that, privet leaves.

The thought of puffing on the contents of Mum's fruit bowl, or attempting to get high from inhaling a cured hedge, was too ridiculous even to consider and was discarded out of hand. Lady Esquire shoe paint was also a heady stimulant, apparently, as was bending over, exhaling and, when all the air in your lungs was expelled, standing up as quickly as you could. This last I did try and can confirm that it offers no benefits whatsoever.

*

On a cold November morning in 1973 – the wedding day of Princess Anne and Captain Mark Phillips, to be precise – Hodgy and myself went off on our bikes to find some work. We turned up at a few farms asking for odd jobs on spec, but to no avail, and were about to give up when we arrived at a scruffy farmhouse up the old Darlington to Stockton railway line. We were greeted by a lean and dishevelled farmer in his thirties. His name was Dave Robinson, and he was dressed in the traditional costume of thick serge pants, checked shirt and a woollen jacket tied around the waist with a piece of rope.

'Do you have any work for us?' I enquired. 'We'll do anything.'

'Reet,' he replied. 'Howay and follow me.'

We followed him into a byre full of pigsties and he led us into one of them. It was filled with piglets and a sow, which he promptly ejected with a swift kick to the behind, leaving the piglets alone with us.

'Get a hold of this 'un like this,' he said, thrusting a piglet's head and forelegs between his thighs with its rear legs held firmly in his hands. He passed the pig back to me and I held it as he took a scalpel and began to slice the little pig's balls in upward strokes until the testicles were out, then with a deft slice he pulled them out, chopped them off and popped them into a stainless-steel dish. I was horrified and barely stifled the urge to gag, forcing it back with a weak smile.

We continued to remove the balls from the rest of the litter, taking turns at holding the animals and chopping them off. The reason for this barbarism was, he explained, that if they weren't removed, he would have a herd of boars that would fight each other to death, resulting in a pork deficit. We were then given shovels and ordered to get rid of several weeks' worth of rotting, stinking pig shit and deposit it on a reeking midden in the yard.

I loved this work and it became my first long-term part-time job. I went up to the farm on weekends and after school – in fact, whenever I could. For this I earned £2 an hour: I was getting rich and was literally as happy as a pig in shit.

Dave, the tenant farmer, lived with his wife in the farmhouse, which was as near a thing as I had seen to a Dickensian hovel – a gloomy, comfortless sitting room containing a couple of thread-bare chairs and a painting of a weeping horse on the wall. Below the central light bulb was a large chest-freezer which contained a whole pig carcass and was covered with a grubby tablecloth.

This had been converted into their dining table and we were invited to join them for soup one lunchtime. The soup, it transpired, was made from the pigs' testicles we had removed, including one that was much larger than the rest.

Had it got into the soup by mistake? Was it indeed a pig's knacker, or had it come from somewhere more sinister? We would never find out. I just could not eat this unsavoury mess and sat staring at it for what seemed like aeons.

'Is it too salty?' enquired the farmer's wife.

'Yes, too salty,' I responded, a little quicker than etiquette should have demanded.

'Sorry,' she said, and she tossed the muck onto the floor, where it was quickly lapped up by a giant black Labrador which suddenly appeared from beneath a pile of bloodied rags in the corner. The rapacious hound tossed the mystery ball up into the air and swallowed it whole: once again I held back the impulse to retch with an insipid grin.

As a replacement for the unsanitary stew, I was offered a bacon sandwich. This was made using inch-and-a-half thick slices of bread, which were covered in a thin layer of anonymous farm smudges. One area featured a clearly identifiable piece of cowpat, with a piece of straw poking out of it. I thanked them and said I would dine outside as it was a nice day. As soon as I had made my exit, I slung it onto the midden, where it lay gently steaming amongst the rest of the sludge. And from that day forward I brought in a packed lunch.

The farm not only kept pigs, but also sheep and cattle, or 'beast' as we called them. Feeding the sheep was a good early morning job. This entailed me desperately clutching onto the bales on the back of the Land Rover so they didn't fall off – which they invariably did, with me beneath them. Another job was to clean out cattle-sheds which had become encrusted with a veritable mountain range of dung over the years. Once my pitchfork had penetrated the recent filth, it released the sulphuric depths of the heap directly into my face. This time the nausea could not be beaten back, and the foul ordure was augmented with my breakfast.

On Saturday and Sunday mornings, I cycled to the farm through icy blizzards. It was so cold that I had to stop every couple of hundred yards to rub my hands together and check to see if my face was still there. I wasn't allowed to catch the bus, as the return journey found me reeking to high heaven and my wretched odour and appearance would have disturbed the other passengers, so it was on the bike that I was forced to travel. Even when I got home, Mum and Dad made me change out of my work clothes in the garage and plunge them into a vat of detergent before I was allowed indoors.

It wasn't all as harrowing as it sounds. There were days when I would drive around as happy as Larry on the old Massey Ferguson tractor wearing the 'tractor coat' – an enormous overcoat made from inch-thick tweed, tied around the waist, once again with a length of rope. I had to take 'pig nuts' and 'cobs' up to the top field on the trailer fixed to the back of the tractor. This was my first attempt at driving anything, and I would slip and slide my way up the field in first gear – urging the brute up the slope in the direction of the top pig field.

When the pigs heard me coming, they'd begin to squeal and snort and snap at each other in anticipation of the grub. At this point, the trick was to get into the field and feed them before they could snaffle up the lot and follow me back out of their field and down to the farm. The first time I did this, I chucked the nuts and cobs off the trailer, turned round and bombed it out through the gate before they could finish. Unfortunately, I misjudged the relative widths of the trailer and the gateposts, and managed to pull down half the fence with me as I passed through.

An old fellow occasionally turned up to work at the farm. He must have been at least a hundred years old and spoke in some distant dialect that few could decipher. When we could make out what he was saying, he generally turned out to be asking topical questions like, 'Is Elvis still at number one in the pops?' or, 'Are them Frenchies up to no good again?'

One day, Hodgy and I knew he was coming up to the farm and decided to give him a fright. We made a mannequin out of old rags we found lying about and took it up to the top of the silo. When we saw him ambling down the lane, Hodgy cried out, 'Goodbye, cruel world!' and hoyed the dummy off the top. The poor old gadgie thought someone was committing suicide, let out a pitiful squeal and buckled over dead – or so we thought.

We climbed down and ran to where he had fallen, but he was already on his feet and apparently none the worse for wear – apart from muttering something about stains.

'Bloody stains,' he kept saying, as he wandered off into a barn to do whatever it was he did. Later, I asked Dave how the old man was and if he had solved the obviously worrying problem of the stains.

'Oh, the stains,' he said. 'I'll have to tidy them up before he kills himself.'

The mystery was solved later, when I found out that the 'stains' were in fact his distinctive local pronunciation of 'stones'. He hadn't even heard or seen our mannequin ruse. He'd just tripped over some loose stones on the track as – it seemed – he did regularly.

*

With all the money I was earning from agriculture, I could live the life of a rich young fool. Accordingly, I blew my wages on records, clothes, going to the pictures and the wrestling.

Tuesday night was wrestling night at the Baths Hall – which was what the Gladstone Baths were called in the winter when the pool had been boarded over to make provision for dances, concerts and, yes, the wrestling. The Victorian stone and wrought-iron hall was the setting for the weekly meetings of minds and brawn that sent the old ladies who attended these tournaments into passionate frenzies. These old biddies turned up in droves – reeking of Horlicks and ready for a fight.

Hodgy and I sat enthralled amongst the aged throng, watching the circus unfold before us. Semi-naked men with names like 'Fat Bill' from Halifax and 'The Welder' – wearing Captain Kirk boots and shorts pulled up to almost nipple height – offered up the entertainment for the early amateur bouts. They were followed by the big guns – Jackie 'Mr TV' Pallo, Gorgeous George, Kendo Nagasaki, Mick McManus, Big Daddy and Giant Haystacks – all presided over by referee Brian Crabtree, brother of Shirley Crabtree a.k.a. Big Daddy.

We always sat on the balcony, where we could get a good view of the ring and – equally important as far as I was concerned – the fuming old ladies who always got ringside seats and sat bellowing and from the off were ready to pounce.

What turned these presumably decent, good-humoured venerable townswomen into raging banshees filled with anger? Were they venting a week's build-up of fury over the seemingly never-ending price increases of Everton Mints? Or was it the tightness of the young men's trousers that sent them into tension-filled fits of pent-up passion – enraged by the blubbery men before them, screaming oaths and slamming their handbags onto the mat, demanding the referee review his opinion or else?

My opinion is that leopards never change their spots, and these seething pensioners were probably exactly the same when they were teenagers, when they would have been cheering on the bear-baiting or the like. The only difference now was that they viewed the tournaments wearing huge great thick astrakhan coats and sporting the standard old ladies' globe hats. The latter, I might add, were sometimes used as gauntlets to be hurled down on the mat in front of particular wrestlers who had incurred their displeasure.

On more than one occasion I have seen a lilac-coloured bulb with several aerials and a flourish of luminous eagles strike fear into the very hearts of the gladiators. I have seen huge men break down and weep when forced to step over a squat, puce and pink, cake-shaped bonnet with a nipple, a net and a nautical emblem, tossed before them in a bellicose fashion by someone old enough to be their grandmother.

One of my favourite wrestlers was Gorgeous George, the narcissistic preener with long, dyed blond hair that he constantly groomed, alternately with his comb and his hands. He would usually finish a bout up-ended with his trunks pulled halfway down, revealing his naked bottom to the old ladies and thereby inciting whoops of fake indignation. When he was released, George would flee – head in one embarrassed hand, the other pulling up his pants – back to the dressing room, where he would presumably put his feet up with a pie and a pint and read the greyhound results.

Another particular favourite was the wrestling vicar. He would turn up in dog collar and surplice, making religious gestures to the crowd as he processed solemnly to the ring. On arrival, he would genuflect in the direction of the referee and say prayers before the first round began. I suspect he was a real vicar, although he had a comedy vicar's voice – a bit like Dick Emery's buck-toothed ecclesiastical character – so who knows? In the world of wrestling, reality and fiction blur seamlessly.

One night we saw the fight of the century, Big Daddy versus Giant Haystacks. It was a monster of a fight that had been built up for weeks and we were excited, though not as excited as the old women. They squawked and bellowed their way into Baths Hall, and fought each other for the best ringside seats. Some had even brought their own incontinence cushions for when the excitement really mounted.

The bout itself was a perfectly choreographed ballet of bulk. The sweat seeped from secret places and the ladies lapped it up, revelling in every grunt and huff. We joined in with the salacious uproar and whooped along, screaming curses at the referee and waving our tins of Peardrax threateningly at him and his judgments. Effectively, it was my first concert – the first time I had felt the excitement of a performance and thrown myself fully into the rush and thrill of it, abandoning all reason and giving in to the power of the spectacle. Like an evangelist, I could do nothing to resist the call of the mighty god of entertainment. I think I then partially understood how the old biddies felt.

After the fight, we nervously approached Giant Haystacks like young fans of a boy-band and stood in front of him, looking up at his towering seven-foot frame and into his hirsute face with its impenetrable stare. As we asked for his autograph, he remained taciturn and unmoving like the man mountain he professed to be, gazing ahead into the distance at something we could not see – perhaps a distant memory, or a simple longing to be back at home in his cave on the outskirts of Barnsley.

We continued to request his signature until he slowly looked down at us and roared an animal-like thundering boom into our faces, his eyes filled with red rage. We shrank back in fear, looking around nervously for an escape route, and then his mood suddenly seemed to lighten.

'All right, lads,' he said, in a kindly light-brown voice, 'give us yer scraps of paper.' We gingerly held them up to him and he signed an 'X'. Then we scuttled away home clutching our pieces of paper, and relived the night on the bus amidst the excited clamour of the senior citizens.

Other nights out were taken at the pictures. My first memory of the flicks was Dad taking me to see *Snow White and the Seven Dwarfs* in Leeds. I recall standing throughout the entire film whilst Dad snoozed through it. Later trips included a tenth birthday treat to see *The King and I*, and a solitary visit to the Saturday morning film club.

This happened one Saturday when, due to foul weather, we didn't climb Helvellyn or there wasn't a rugby match on. Friends had told me how great these mornings were and what I was missing, so this really was a treat. How disappointed I was. The venue for the film club was the ABC cinema on North Road. Within was a seething mass of uncontrolled youths – hurling rolled-up programmes at each other and running up and down the aisles – with the cinema manager in tears on the stage, trying to save his picture house from demolition at the hands of the town's tearaways.

When a minimal degree of civility had been restored, the movies began. First came a *Felix the Cat* cartoon, followed by an episode of *Flash Gordon* which ended up melting in front of our eyes to the contemptuous cheers of the audience. Then came a British Children's Film Foundation feature, with some young refugees scurrying about in Norfolk beneath swaying poplar trees to the music of Benjamin Britten.

The plot was instantly forgettable – probably something about saving a tree containing the nest of the last blue-titted fen warbler in England, or the discovery of a barn containing a family of traditional gypsies with a pet monkey – and the crumminess of the picture led to condescending cries of disdain from the kids, followed, once again, by a serious explosion of rioting. This time, food came into the equation. Ice-cream tubs and bits of bread migrated south towards the screen, and the manager appeared once again, now waving a tennis racket in a vain attempt to save his precious screen from the flying comestibles. He heroically batted away the contents of lunchboxes whilst wiping away his tears with his handkerchief, probably wishing he had a rifle or, failing that, a noose.

That was the only time I went to the Saturday morning pictures. However the release of a new Ray Harryhausen was always a valid reason to skive off school. *The Seventh Voyage of Sinbad* was unbeatable with its monsters and mythical beasts, as was *The Golden Voyage of Sinbad*. In fact, any voyage that Sinbad undertook, I would be there rooting for him.

Then came the X films. Some school-friends had already crept in the back door of the pictures to see an X-rated movie, but there'd been nothing so far that had really taken my fancy, until the opening of *Don't Look Now* with Donald Sutherland and Julie Christie. This looked scary, and well worth the gamble of trying to look eighteen to get in, even though we were clearly nowhere near that age.

Our objective of spurious maturity was pursued in the following ways:

(a) standing on tiptoes at the box office;
(b) trying to lower our voices by an octave while adopting the accent of the local doctor;
(c) assuming a stony face with one eyebrow raised, giving us the air of visiting academics, here to give the film serious critical appraisal.

Being taller, thicker-set and generally older-looking, the task of buying the tickets was given to Hodgy.

'Two seats in the stalls, please,' he gravely growled with a look of acute earnestness on his face, as if he were planning a route up the Eiger.

'Certainly sir,' came the reply, and we were in.

We emerged from *Don't Look Now* as quivering wrecks. Terror had weakened us to our very cores, and as we parted to go our separate ways home, I was convinced I saw scuttling red dwarfs up every back alley. After weeks of nightmares, I decided to inflict more punishment on myself and went to see *The Wicker Man*. Fortunately, this quite laughable film was as devoid of terror then as it is now.

I was getting used to this X-film business, but things went awry when a gang of us tried to get into *Enter the Dragon* with Bruce Lee. Martial arts fever had gripped the nation's youth thanks to David Carradine in TV's *Kung Fu* series, wherein he played a tranquil ex-Shaolin monk who would get into scrapes with local landowners in cowboy-land, resulting in him being forced to employ his fighting skills to defeat all and sundry. Unfortunately, you had to wait until the end of each episode before seeing him have his scrap. But apparently in *Enter the Dragon*, Bruce Lee went for it hell for leather from start to finish, and so off we went to see it, full of confidence.

The first three of us got in easily, until the fourth kid asked for a child's half ticket and we were rumbled – our tickets were refunded and we were thrown out onto the street, where we demonstrated the skills of the Shaolin monks on the fourth kid until he begged for mercy. No worries though, we simply sneaked in round the back and saw the film for free.

About this time, Peter Sellers's *The Pink Panther* was showing across the land, and a big fuss was being made about it. One notable manifestation of the film's impressive marketing budget was the deployment of out-of-work actors dressed in Pink Panther costumes to hand out leaflets for the movie on high streets. I came across one of these costumed troupers on the High Row one day as he went about his work. Some ignorant young simpleton was in the process of setting fire to his tail with a lighter, and the poor man inside didn't know what to do. Should he continue with his performance, or tear off the costume and run before he was burnt alive? He opted for neither. Instead he turned to his assailant, and from within the Pink Panther's head came a muffled but clearly audible 'Fuck off'.

CHAPTER
TWELVE

'The mysteries of the past were everywhere, but ever so slightly dressed in mid-70s colours'

At this time, I was searching ever further afield in my endless quest for musical satisfaction. East of Eden's 'Jig a Jig' and Lindisfarne's 'Meet Me On The Corner' had pointed me in the direction of folk-rock and Fairport Convention. This stuff fitted in nicely with my twin fascinations with history and the countryside. I also, following his appearance on *Top of the Pops*, loved Robert Wyatt's version of 'I'm a Believer', which in turn led me to explore some of the more obscure hippy/jazz bands like Henry Cow and Gong.

At school it was still The Faces and Free who loomed largest in my repertoire of rock fandom. At least I could have conversations about these groups – no one else was willing to discuss David Allen's pot-head pixie hats or Fred Frith's crocodile-clip guitar technique, and I was still quite happy mouthing Andy Fraser from Free's bass solo from the live version of 'Mr Big'. This came from the new live album by Free, Free Live – still, to my mind, the best live album ever recorded. I would lie in bed at night playing it on the little Dansette and imagining that I was there at the concert.

In an English lesson with Miss Ayres, we had been asked to write about a piece of music that moved us or painted a picture in our minds, and she played us some inspiring examples for the less imaginative to follow — classical pieces like 'Peter and The Wolf' and Wagner's 'Ride of the Valkyries'. I decided to give a presentation about Free's 'My Brother Jake'.

I'm still not entirely sure what this song is about even now, although I think it may refer to Paul Kossoff's increasing drug dependency and Paul Rodgers's suggestion that he'd be better off giving up the dope. But in my mind 'My Brother Jake' referred to singer Paul Rodgers's imaginary mentally deficient brother who couldn't get a grip on life and required guidance to help him through every day. Lines like 'My brother Jake, head, down, it's a scrapin' the ground' were taken literally and described as such in my piece.

A car-jack and trolley had to be employed to help the poor, sick Jake make his way. Likewise, Jake could not 'stay away', and special medical attention was needed for this affliction, not to mention the fact that when he went out he didn't 'have to know what the world's about'. Yes, it was very clear from these lyrics that Jake was severely mentally disabled, and so it was that I described him in my essay. I even accompanied it with a drawing of the wretched and pitiful creature, and Miss Ayres, unable to decipher the lyrics herself, had to concede and applaud my valiant and sympathetic effort.

On another occasion, Miss Ayres asked us to describe a concert, and once again offered us images of baton-waving conductors and oafish tuba players working their way through 'Land of Hope and Glory'. I decided to lie, and give a blow-by-blow description of

The Faces at Newcastle City Hall – an event which I pretended to have attended just the previous week.

The whole gig was described in intense detail just as I thought it might have taken place – from sitting down in the hall, to the entrance of the band, right through to the finale and seeing Miss Heaton getting into a limousine with Rod Stewart. Years later, I was to feel a real stab of jealousy when I found out that my good friend and colleague Bob Mortimer (who was lucky enough to have older brothers to accompany him) did actually attend this performance.

I loved English, but art lessons were my favourite. This was largely thanks to our young and rather bohemian art teacher Mr Welsh, who, having a modern approach to pedagogy, allowed us to call him by his first name, which was Dick. Our little art gang numbered myself, Rod Willcox, Steve Parry and Mike Nelson, and Dick allowed us to bring our records in and play them during class.

I brought in In Search Of Space by Hawkwind and painted endless pictures of spacecraft circling planets. In fact, I designed my own spaceship, which looked uncannily like a Ford Transit van minus the wheels, and this became my trademark – appearing somewhere in every painting I did. Even if it was an exercise in crosshatching, my spaceship would be there somewhere hidden within the diagram.

Dick was a mid-twenties groover with cool specs and collar-length wavy blond hair, who would tell us stories of his extra-curricular activities as we painted. He once told us of an idea he had for a painting that came to him at home in bed in his flat. As he lay staring at the ceiling, a collection of images appeared

— swirls of colour, distorted cartoon faces and spears of light shot out of the walls at him. What an imagination he has, we thought, only years later wondering if perhaps his imaginative vision had been expanded by stimulants such as light ale or strong coffee.

One day, Rod, Steve and me were sent off to sketch a land-scape within the school grounds. We found a shady area beneath a rowan tree and proceeded to draw. Rod and Steve began to try and capture the playing fields whilst I brazenly disregarded Dick's requests and did a detailed picture of a discarded plastic cup, intri-cately drawn with fine shading and my spaceship hovering above it.

As we sat sketching, we discussed our respective hair lengths and how long they might be by the time we left school. Rod's hair was the longest in our little group — cascading over his shoulders in thick brown waves, and as we sat, he announced that he was considering getting it cut into a 'shaggy' style by his sister who was a hairdresser, thereby retaining the length, yet giving it a more current appeal. Yes, it would be so. He would go and see his sister at lunchtime and return in the afternoon with a startling new cut, and all the girls would flock around him adoringly.

Lunchtime came and went as we awaited Rod's return, and it was looking as if he wouldn't appear at all when suddenly there he stood, resplendent at the classroom door with a silky-stranded bubble-perm. The whole class erupted with laughter.

His sister was a hairdresser, it was true, and a good one, but she had never done men's hair, and she had given Rod a terrific modern ladies' do, and had primped and sprayed it into the most architecturally dynamic hairstyle the school — nay, the town — had ever seen. Rod fled in total embarrassment and was last seen

171

tearing through the school gates followed by a cloud of hairspray and a flock of birds wishing to nest in his coiffured curls.

The next day, Rod returned to school with the longer tendrils lopped off and the perm relaxed into a still voluminous but acceptable mound. 'You look like Don McLean,' I barked.

'Yes,' he returned defensively, 'that's exactly what I wanted, I love Don McLean and I like his hair, so that's what I got.' And from then on, to justify his haircut, he brought 'American Pie' into the art rooms to accompany our painting lessons. This only lasted a few weeks though, until he realised that Jon Anderson from Yes had a similar cut and 'American Pie' was exchanged for Tales From Topographic Oceans.

Rod, Steve and me were invited to paint the backdrop for a production of *The Good Old Days* that the drama department was putting on, and we painted tall-hatted Victorian men accompanying parasol-wielding ladies through streets filled with horses and carriages and – if you looked very carefully – a transit van-shaped spaceship peeping out from behind a chimney sweep. With this masterpiece completed, we were to operate the spotlights on the night from the balconies, and this we did to the worst of our abilities.

The drama group had spent weeks rehearsing, but we thought we could enhance the show with our comical use of the spotlights by pretending we didn't know whose line was next. The spots would career all around the stage until they landed on someone who didn't have a line; they would then look around startled, wondering whether they had a line or not, while the actor who did have the line looked equally confused, all while we sat in the balcony laughing hysterically at our hilarious work.

We stopped laughing in the interval, when we were dragged

from our perches and hauled over the coals by all of the teachers involved in the production. How dare we jeopardise the performance with our childish and self-indulgent use of lights? We had better not muck about in the second act or we would have the spots firmly rammed up our arses and switched on, and then we would see who was laughing. These threats had the ring of conviction about them, and for the rest of the show we follow-spotted the performers carefully and in grim silence.

*

At home, after school, I continued with my artwork – painting pictures of my spaceship and experimenting with my new hobby, which was embroidery. Having raided Mum's sewing box one day in search of something to alleviate the boredom, I came across a selection of silken embroidery threads and set to work on the back of my Levi's denim jacket. The outcome was a large green and red interpretation of Hawkwind's twin-headed eagle, right across the back.

I liked this very much, and set to work on the front of the jacket. This time I detailed a rainbow over the pocket, while around the bottom of the jacket, in various colours, I stitched Hendrix, Free, King Crimson and Yes.

Going out wearing my sumptuously adorned jacket, I was inundated with requests to work on other garments for cash – a welcome extension of my earlier haversack-based employment – and this I did: sewing the names of bands onto people's jeans and coats, until I developed such awful calluses on my fingers that I was forced to stop – but not before I had made a mark in the world of needlecraft.

Handicrafts played a large part in the life of the Moir family. Mum and Dad had been running a kind of cottage industry for a while now. This involved Dad creating wooden works of art in the garage/decontamination tank, and Mum painting them. Dad had always been handy with wood, and had been knocking up furniture, Christmas presents and surfboards for as long as I could remember. He once made a trailer that transformed into a tented caravan when a lever was pulled. This contraption worked very well and was deployed on many a trip to the Lakes, the Dales, or the Solway Firth.

Anyway, Dad had bought a wood-turning machine from one of his friends at work, and had begun to turn plates and vases on it. Mum then employed her painterly skills to adorn the assorted wooden things with tiny oil paintings of flowers.

After a while, the house began to fill up with these ornaments and *objets d'art* and friends and relations had been used up as receptacles for the overflow. So it was decided to set up stall at weekend craft fairs, hopefully to get rid of them there and make some extra money on the side.

And they did very well. In market squares, in villages, up hill and down dale alongside other bearded, pipe-smoking, Arran sweater-wearing folksingers and others who plied the trades of yesteryear, they sold bowls and light-pulls, jewellery boxes and brooches, and even whipping tops for the kiddies.

Whilst Mum and Dad and Lois were away at the fairs, I was down at the old town dump with my friend Steve Parry. Steve was in my class at school and was one of us hairies, with an older brother, Dick, who appeared very enigmatic with his long mousy hair, oily overalls, Black Sabbath albums and three years' extra experience of life. For some reason Dick always seemed to look rather baffled, but maybe this was just his way of looking cool to us young pups.

Steve and Dick lived alone with their mum in a little cul-de-sac off Geneva Road. I don't know if their dad had died or had simply disappeared, but it was a rare thing at this time to have a friend with only one parent present. And their mum clearly had her hands full with her two boys.

Steve, normally mild-mannered and quiet, would turn into a screaming dervish at home. He and his mum would yell at each other the whole time. When we stepped outside the house, though, he'd turn to me and say, 'Sorry about that,' in a calm, soft voice, and serenity would return.

On town-dump mornings I would rise at 6am, get on my bike and ride round to Steve's house, have a cup of tea whilst civil war erupted around me, and then we'd ride off together towards the tip.

Steve and I looked pretty similar. We both had shoulder-length mousy blond hair, and both wore suede boots, cheesecloth shirts, Levi's jeans and jackets with Hawkwind embroidered on the back – his a poorer version of mine (the reason being that I did it myself and, as he was a friend, did it for free; quicker and without quite the care and attention I gave my own). And off we'd head on our racing bikes, with spades tied to the crossbars and carrying canvas bags filled with newspaper. 'Why?' I hear you speculate. Here's why.

On the outskirts of Darlington, on the road to Croft, quite near a place called 'Hells Kettles' (bottomless pits filled with water which were said to have inspired Lewis Carroll's *Alice in Wonderland*, Lewis being a local), was the old Victorian town tip. Now an overgrown mound, this antique refuse facility was bursting at the seams with ancient treasure, and we were there to dig it up. Most of the bottles and stone jars we found were fairly worthless, but we loved them anyway. And there were rarities too: Codds bottles (origin of the phrase 'codswallop'), or, if you were very lucky, a blue or amber spirit bottle.

Whilst digging up the past we sang folk-rock songs, pausing only to eat bread and cheese and suck on small bottles of cider as they must have done a hundred years ago on this site. Although they would probably have thought us deranged for digging up their rubbish.

At this time, there was a general feeling everywhere you looked of reaching back into the past and searching for a lost England that was somehow a better and simpler place to live, whether it was via music, bottles, or even Mum and Dad at the craft fairs. Or 'fayres' as they were always misspelt in an attempt to suggest that the items on sale were made using ancient and lost skills, and were therefore superior to today's mass-produced stuff – which, in most cases, they were.

The mysteries of the past were everywhere, but ever so slightly dressed in mid-'70s colours. This trend began in the 1960s with Portobello market antiques and Sergeant Pepper, but then turned more rural in the 1970s, with working-class Victorian clothes being in vogue, and pop stars wanting to live in the country and pretend to be farmers … It wasn't a marketing ploy by anyone in particular, just a sort of mass feeling throughout the nation – a sense of trying to get back to the earth now we had indulged ourselves in the '50s and '60s postwar plastic explosion.

Even Led Zeppelin were doing folk songs and driving to

stadium gigs on tractors, and wearing old tweed jackets, grandad shirts and flat caps. I, of course, took it to extremes and whenever I could, attempted to emulate a Victorian way of life.

I had Mum make me a stripy winceyette nightshirt and nightcap, which I would wear to bed each night carrying a candle and candleholder like Wee Willy Winkie up into my bedroom, where I read a Dickens novel by candlelight before dropping off into a deep slumber and dreaming of shire horses and flagons of ale.

Eventually, the garage began to fill up with old bottles and something had to be done with them. The answer was easy. I would give them to Mum and Dad to sell on the stall at the craft fairs. And so I did – adding another string to my financial bow. They didn't bring in a lot of cash, but me being the young entrepreneur I was, every little counted.

CHAPTER THIRTEEN

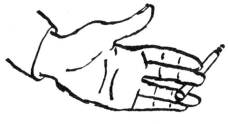

vulcan salute
style

'It wasn't all furze-cutting and feeding baby lambs in a pre-Raphaelite mist'

Meanwhile, back at the farm . . .

There were two ways of getting to the place which was still my most important source of income. One was to cycle up Yarm Road, and the other was to go up the old – now disused – Darlington to Stockton railway. The world's first railway line was now just a narrow cinder track, banked by undergrowth and hawthorn bushes, and it was in this undergrowth that I discovered an ancient relic.

Cycling to the farm one day, I paused to destroy an ants' nest with a stick. Beating the living daylights out of the mound, I saw something half-buried in the scrub and decided to investigate. It was a stone marker-post from the original railway in 1825, carved with a pair of arrows and the mileage between Darlington and Stockton.

I had discovered a major historical artefact. I was like Howard Carter discovering Tutankhamun's sarcophagus and I would become famous and rich beyond the dreams of Croesus. I looked around, no one was about, and so I covered the stone and marked the site with a stick, so I could return to it later with a crack team of archaeologists, the mayor and a TV crew. Off I went to work, secure in the secret knowledge that I was on the brink of fame and fortune.

Further down the track, looking over a fence into a field, I saw what at first appeared to be a giant peach beside a hay bale. Then it moved, and I saw that it was a human in a state of semi-undress. I briefly concealed myself behind a thicket in order to spy on the person, and it turned out to be a stocky girl of about fifteen, relieving herself in the field. She hoiked up her trousers and ran off in the direction of a hovel.

I carried on my way, and the unsightly image eventually vanished from my mind. Ten minutes later, the same thing happened. There she was, squatting in a field, her voluminous rear exposed to the elements. Was she incontinent, or was this display for my benefit? A kind of animalistic lure to tempt me into her domain with a view to mating? It certainly seemed that way, and I was sure she knew I was there. I grew concerned and sped onward to the farm.

On arrival, I told the farmer of the bulky lass I had seen crouching in the corn field and he said, 'Oh her, she's always doing that – she thinks it'll make the lads like her.' Whether any of the lads did like her I don't know. I'm sure a few of them did 'like' her on more than one occasion, but I most certainly wasn't going to 'like' her, even though I kept getting regular glimpses out of the corner of my eye of the portly mystery girl squatting in a distant pasture trying to entice me with her huge unvarnished bald arse.

Working on the farm gave me a sense of bucolic joy. I was a ruralist and could till the land and tend the beasts whilst singing my newly learnt repertoire of folk songs like a character from a Thomas Hardy novel. But it wasn't all furze-cutting and feeding baby lambs in a pre-Raphaelite mist. In fact, it was nothing like that whatsoever. In reality it was filthy, grim and sometimes horrific.

On one occasion, I was given the monumentally disturbing task of destroying a piglet that was spastic and needed to be killed before it was slowly eaten to death by its siblings and mother. I was shown the quickest and most humane method of dispatching the little pig, and this meant taking a gripe, or pitchfork, placing one of the prongs on its temple, and with a firm and deft stroke of the boot, plunging the spear into its brain.

I was left alone with the piglet and the gripe and my conscience, feeling incapable of delivering such a murderous blow. It lay there, twisted and corrupt, its little body twitching from the constant spasms, and I spent at least half an hour looking at it and giving it its last rites, and telling it how sorry I was that I had to do this terrible deed.

Then, as quickly as I could, I placed the gripe on its head and thrust it in. The tiny body stopped its twitching and lay there with my tears falling onto it. It was me who was shaking now, but I managed to convince myself that I had done the right thing, and solemnly carried the lifeless body back to the farmer, whereupon he took it like an old rag and unceremoniously hurled it onto the midden for the crows and cats to dispose of.

Another revolting sight I would later witness was a vet performing an autopsy on two large Landrace sows that had caught pneumonia and died. He drilled two large holes into the pigs' bellies and examined their guts. This image was bad enough, but worse was yet to come.

Later in the day, as the carcasses began to fester while awaiting a trailer to take them away, I cast an eye over the corpses and saw movement from within. And then, from out of the holes the vet had made, emerged two kittens that had been frolicking inside the dead pigs, and were covered in blood and pus and other diverse unpleasantnesses. I stemmed a cascade of vomit and wondered if there were any folk songs from Cecil Sharpe's Songs of Old England that covered such diabolical scenes. Somehow, I doubted it.

There were, of course, plenty of high points and moments of fun to be had: riding pigs around the fields, for example, was a hoot. However, our hog rodeo was not always the carefree entertainment we might have wished for. One day as we rode the beasts, we heard the most horrendous banging coming from one of the old railway carriages which were used to house some of the pigs out in the field. Following the source of the sound, the end of one of the carriages was buckling under the pressure of a boar inside, ramming itself at the wall in an attempt to escape, which it did in a dramatic explosion of splintering wood and metal.

These monsters were incredibly powerful and this brute was more dynamic than most. It ran squealing and roaring around the field, and we heard the farmer screaming for us to catch it. Catch a demonic leviathan like that? But how? There was only one way, it soon became clear to us. We must employ martial arts; Kung Fu was the only way to curb its rampage. We charged around the field making Bruce Lee-style squeals and leaping through the air – arms and legs flailing – but to no avail, we could not stop the voyage of the porcine behemoth.

We were watched with great disappointment by the farmer, who, with shaking head, showed us the correct way to halt the advance of a 600lb animal. He took a length of thick twine, formed it into a lasso, and stealthily crept up in front of the boar offering gentle words of encouragement. Then he pounced, hooking the rope over its two lower tusks. Realising what had happened, the pig automatically began to pull back, and was then swiftly tied to a gatepost.

Even once its back legs were tethered, the brute still kept pulling, and was in danger of lacerating its mouth. So the farmer took a brick and smashed off the tusks, which went flying through the air into some distant corner of the field, never to be seen again. We knew this for a fact as we spent the rest of the day trying to find them to make a necklace.

That evening, when I arrived home and had done my feculence-inspired quarantine in the garage, I told Dad about my archaeological discovery on the railway line and asked how I should proceed with it. He said he knew a chap at work who was familiar with such things and would speak to him. This he did, and within a couple of days the chap in question appeared on the front of the *Northern Echo* proudly displaying my discovery. The swine had dug it up and taken the credit, handing it over to the town museum where it was displayed in pride of place with his name beneath it as the finder.

It was not the only discovery that I made – and though the second was of a less obviously historic nature, it was still not without long-term consequences. Taking a stroll with Mum and Lois one evening I came across a full packet of cigarettes. 'Ooh look,' I exclaimed, 'a full packet of fags – shall I keep them?'

Mum – best intentions to the fore, as ever – invited me to try one, declaring confidently that if I did I would find it revolting and never smoke again. I took her up on this offer, but unfortunately her plan backfired, as the cigarettes were a minty menthol flavour and not at all unpalatable, and this episode set me off on the filthy road of the smoker.

I had begun to attend the Methodist youth club on Yarm Road, and these evenings began with a heathen prelude in the form of a trip to the tobacconist, where a single cigarette could be bought for a penny, and five of us would make a joint investment in a bottle of Woodpecker cider. The latter was consumed around the back of the club, giving us the Dutch courage required to ask a girl to dance once inside, while puffing on the cigarette would, we felt, give us the appearance of young sophisticates.

A number of smoking techniques could be employed, which were successfully put into practice by older boys and men, and emulated by us novices. There was the 'inside the hand' method developed by outdoor workers to stop the wind burning the fag down too quickly, this also having the benefit of keeping the palm of the hand warm in cold weather. The 'thumb and forefinger' style was favoured by ruffians and tough guys. The strangely provocative 'Vulcan salute' method was used by oddballs and people wishing to make an impression.

Then there was the Rolling Stone 'stick it in your mouth and leave it there' gambit, and finally the 'right at the root of the index and middle finger' approach. I went for the traditional 'index and middle finger' style, although I ornamented this by holding it at mouth level at all times in the style of Noel Coward or Bet Lynch, making me appear louche and charismatic.

Fags extinguished and cider quaffed, we made our way into the youth club and took our positions against the wall opposite the girls. Dancing was a precarious business, as the style amongst most boys at the time was to thrust your hands deep into your pockets and kick your legs out at various angles whilst looking nonplussed and bored.

This meant that you never looked where you were going and might at any moment trip up over a loose handbag. Because your hands were jammed into your pockets, there was no way of removing them in sufficient time to break your fall. St John's Ambulance was always on standby and A&E departments were often filled in the evenings with boys with broken noses.

Fortunately I found this style of dancing ludicrous and developed my own brand of choreography which involved plenty of arm-waving and emulation of animals – like the duck walk or a movement somewhat akin to a foraging ape. This did not find much favour with the ladies, but I was at least tolerated and even found faintly amusing by most of them.

There was a split appearing amongst the youth. The boys who enjoyed the hands in pockets style of dancing wore Oxford bags and would soon be heading towards Wigan Casino for Northern Soul weekends. I, on the other hand, was destined for Reading Festival and the land of the hairies. But at this stage the rift was in its infancy and we all thrashed about together regardless.

On my way home one night from the club, I heard the roar of a powerful engine coming tearing towards me. It must be a Lamborghini, I thought, or some kind of demonic Italian super-car. Then, over the brow of a hill came a small, light-blue invalid car, or 'spacka-chariot', as we rather insensitively called them. I dimly recalled talk of this vehicle, and remembered Dad having claimed to see it tearing along at 90mph ...

Subsequent investigations revealed that the owner had taken out the maker's engine and replaced it with that of a 1600 GT

Ford Cortina which he had somehow managed to shoehorn into the tiny car. I later heard that he was arrested and the mean machine impounded, which was a shame as I don't think it was really doing any harm, and it certainly added a touch of maverick distinction to Darlington's road system. Especially with that vulture perched on its wing mirror.

Back at home, I was spending my evenings listening to prog rock whilst embroidering and painting. On one occasion – as my mother has kindly mentioned already – I did a painting of Marc Bolan and sent it in to *Jackie* magazine under my sister's name, where it was printed, winning me a handsome prize of £5. The kudos was not forthcoming, however, as I didn't want my friends to know I read girls' comics.

Another time, I won a competition on the back of a Kellogg's Cornflakes packet to paint a scene which conjured up the essence of that trusty breakfast cereal. Sadly, the exact nature of the reward accrued by my touching bucolic landscape of a combine harvester at work now escapes me.

*

For all these successful ventures into the art world, there was still something missing from my life. I needed to join in with the music I was listening to – I needed a musical instrument. After much deliberation I decided on a set of drums. This was, of course, without discussing the matter with my parents.

Eventually, I broached the tricky subject and to my surprise this rash proposal was agreed to, with one stipulation. I could only play the drums on Saturday afternoons when Mum and Dad had gone out, and then only in the garage, and very quietly at that.

Rod Willcox had been playing the drums for a while now and so he was definitely the right person to ask about acquiring some. It just so happened that he had a Premier kit that he was getting rid of in favour of a new Pearl outfit, and so I greedily accepted his price of £5. The set included a bass drum, snare and a hi-hat – it was basic, but all I needed to make a row with.

The only problem was that I was utterly rhythmless. In Mr Shepherd's school music lessons I had been relegated to the back of the class with the triangle and told that I had no talent in this field whatsoever, and should never ever attempt music in any form under penalty of death. And so there I was, in charge of a professional and devastatingly loud piece of musical instrumentation, with absolutely no idea what to do with it.

Rod kindly taught me the rudiments of percussion, of which the basic drum roll was the only thing I could actually grasp – perhaps because it required no actual sense of rhythm. On the days when practice was forbidden I would sit on my bed happily rolling my sticks around the drums' skin until I finally achieved a reasonably coherent effect.

Saturday afternoons were another matter. I set the kit up in the garage and hammered away sounding like a herd of cows descending a tin staircase until the police arrived with riot shields and insisted that I desist for the sake of the neighbours' mental health. The drum kit's days were numbered. I needed a subtler and more responsive instrument.

CHAPTER
FOURTEEN

'There was something else peculiar: on every table stood a whippet'

While I waited eagerly for my musical destiny to reveal itself, water-based activities continued to provide a pleasurable diversion. Hodgy's dad Dennis had built us a blue canvas two-man kayak, and we would canoe down the Tees in the early evenings, pretending we were in Vietnam. The war over there was drawing to a close and was featured on the news fairly regularly, so it felt prudent to keep a lookout for Vietcong guerrillas as we drifted gently down the river with its overhanging trees and mayflies dancing across the water. Perhaps we might even get a glimpse of Pol Pot peeping out of a vole-hole in the river bank.

On one occasion, we took our canoe to Ullswater and paddled the entire eleven miles, pausing only for tomato sandwiches on a small island halfway along. Shortly after this I began to take proper canoeing lessons. These took place in the school swimming pool and enabled me – along with several other aquatically inclined characters from around the region – to learn Eskimo rolls, hand rolls, sculling, the lot.

One of these other canoeists was a chap from Crook called Peter who had a very high-pitched Durham accent and said everything very clearly and precisely, like a child reading out something they had written with stops in between each word.

'I. Am. Going. To. Sail. Across. The. Baths. Right. Now,' he would declare proudly, and then do just what he had predicted, invariably collapsing into the water with a long, high-pitched 'Oooooooohhhhh'. I would later use Peter's voice for the characters called The Stotts in *Big Night Out*. But for the moment I had become proficient enough at canoeing to go white-water slaloming on the River Swale at Richmond, and was soon pushing the canoe down thin gullies with water tearing down them at some speed, shooting rapids and hurtling over waterfalls.

When I wasn't doing this, I was learning scuba-diving. Around this time, the moment came to go and see the careers officer in order to try and work out what I might do on leaving. He asked what sports I enjoyed and I replied 'canoeing and scuba'. His instantaneous response was 'Navy, next!' and I was tossed out into the corridor believing I had just enlisted.

I hadn't, of course, and I was still none the wiser about what I wanted to do when I eventually left school. I did quite fancy art college, but I dared not raise the subject, as I knew it would cost money that Mum and Dad didn't have. Well, I did mention it once, but Dad just batted around the subject and tried to persuade me to get a job that earned money and do art in my spare time.

Earning money was something I didn't have a problem with. You would think the farmwork, the haversacks, the embroidery and the bottle sales would have been enough for me, but they weren't. So when I was offered a job delivering milk, I took it, even though it meant rising at 5.30am every day and squeezing into the back of a tiny van full of milk crates with two other boys.

One of these boys was called Donald Pew, whom we cruelly nicknamed Donald 'Poo' as his clothes always smelt of putrid milk. Poor little Don's mum never washed his clothes and therefore, as the milky mornings extended their clammy welcomes to his outfit, he gradually became unbearably noxious. Donald also wore glasses and one of the lenses had fallen out so his mum had repaired them with Sellotape which, over the years, had turned yellow.

Poor, poor Don. We once picked him up after he hadn't been able to get into his house and we found him sleeping under the hedge outside his home. This poignant individual was the closest I'd ever get to encountering a Dickensian urchin. But the poignant novelty of his acquaintance was not a strong enough draw to keep me in the job. The milk round was unbearable and poorly paid, and it meant I was late for school every day, so I packed it in sharpish.

Although I didn't know it, my time at the farm was also coming to a close. Hodgy was a big, burly lad and ideally constructed for agricultural labour. I, on the other hand, was five foot eleven inches tall and weighed nine stone, and was therefore not cut out for farm work at all (even though I loved doing it). I was designed more for cleaning the insides of drainpipes, or working for a lookalike agency as a knitting needle.

The main cloud on my employment horizon was the fact that Hodgy could carry two hundredweight bags of grain at a time – whereas I could only manage one. The farmer was under instruc-

My Brother Jake
(page 169)

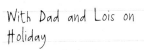

With Dad and Lois on
Holiday

Victorian way of life
(page 176)

Mum chasing me down the street (page 199)

Manhair and Quiff the barber's (page 251)

Above: Me looking sullen,
fifth from the left on the
back row

Whippet on the table
(page 200)

V.W. BEETLE

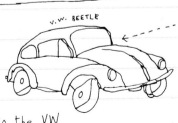

Smashing into the VW
Beetle (page 214)

Mr Brown's Truss
(page 224)

THE TRUSS

Me with Jon Irvine
(page 234)

The egg-shaped ghost
(page 233)

Jackson   Gilligan

The Workshop

Egg shaped ghost.

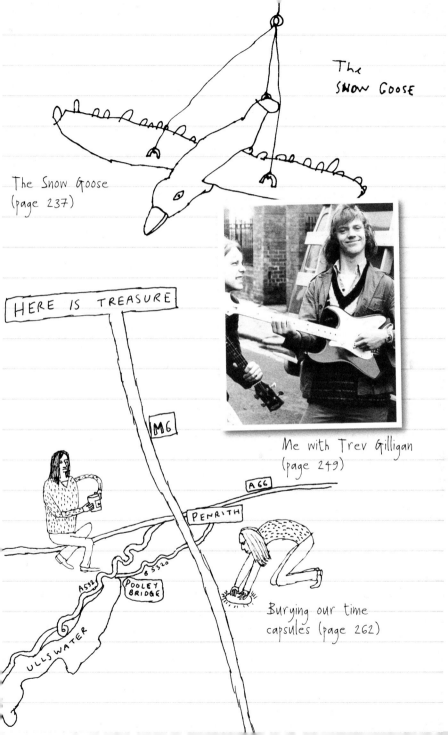

The Snow Goose
(page 237)

The
SNOW GOOSE

HERE IS TREASURE

M6

A66

PENRITH

A592

B5320

POOLEY
BRIDGE

ULLSWATER

Me with Trev Gilligan
(page 249)

Burying our time
capsules (page 262)

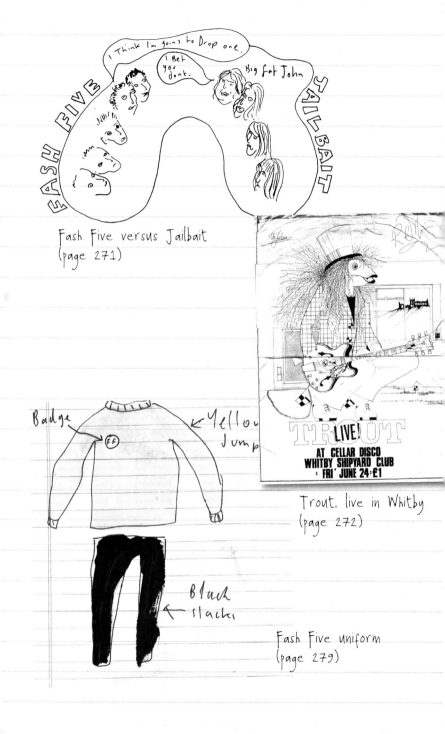

Fash Five versus Jailbait
(page 271)

Trout, live in Whitby
(page 272)

Fash Five uniform
(page 279)

The Fash Five salute
(page 279)

My Calling Card (page 278)

The Morris Traveller
(page 281)

Me shopping for records

The red
chelsea boot
with cuban
heel.

The Red Chelsea b[oot]
(page 284)

Gavin the Fashionable Bear

Gavin the fashionable bear
(page 254)

tions to cut his labour force in half, and it was clear which half would have to go. And so, with a heavy heart and a tear in my eye, I was dismissed.

I took my wages and blew them at a new shop in town. The place was called Guru and it stocked everything anyone needed to look like you'd just stepped out of Haight-Ashbury in 1967 or, indeed, if you wanted to look like a hobbit. I decided on a combination of the two. So I bought a pair of Levi's loons with more patches than anyone had ever seen before, a velvet mirrored scoop-neck T-shirt, and a sort of brown and purple hessian coat that I drenched in patchouli oil, and accessorised with a selection of beads and Hendrix badges.

Thus I overcame my disappointment at being fired from the farm, and sloped off home in my carefully careless garments. Whilst in Guru, I also bought some Strawberry Fields joss sticks and took them into school along with my new Bad Company album, so my friends and I could discuss the merits of Paul Rodgers's new band whilst bathing in the sweet aroma of Asian fruit.

This important ritual took place round the back of the sports equipment hut by the walled field, and it wasn't long before some young informer had told a teacher that we were up to no good. It wasn't much longer before we were hauled into the headmaster Mr Bryant's office, and accused of taking drugs.

'Ah, you mean the joss sticks,' I announced cockily, knowing there had been a terrible mistake.

'Yes, that's exactly what I mean,' came the reply. 'I will not tolerate drugs on these premises, and the matter will have to be handed over to the police.' He wouldn't budge, no matter how much I tried to tell him that they were simply ambient incense sticks, similar to the stuff used in the Catholic Church.

It was then that a younger teacher came into the office and a few whispered words were exchanged. Mr Bryant turned to us and said, 'Very well, it seems I was wrong, but I do not want to see any of you in possession of these disgusting perfumed rods again. Now get out.' And that's how the most innocent of fragrant sticks were banned from school.

My love life was still fairly nonexistent. In fact it was completely nonexistent. Then I got word of a girl who had taken an interest in me. Her name was Mandy and she was in the fifth year, which meant she was a woman. This was scary, and things got even more alarming when I found out that her nickname was 'Randy' Mandy. Although I'm sure a lot of Mandies are nick-named 'Randy' whether they are randy or not. Anyway, it turned out that this one was. Randy, that is. Frighteningly so.

As she was in the fifth year, I decided I had better make an effort at a first date, and we decided to meet at a country pub like adults do. I had been in pubs with Mum and Dad, but this was a first for me and the whole thing turned me into a shivering wreck. Anyway, I arrived at the pub early and waited outside for Mandy to arrive, which she duly did, wearing a huge white fur coat and white platforms that made her not only two inches taller than me, but also twice as wide.

We went into the pub – her looking like a giant cumulus cloud and me the spitting image of Bilbo Baggins. After successfully ordering two halves of shandy, we sat beside the log fire and felt very grown up. Conversation was horribly strained and revolved mainly around the quality of the fire and where, we wondered, did the logs come from? When the shandies were drained – which took all of four minutes – I made a lame excuse about having to get off home and revise.

As we left the pub and stood at the bus stop, I began to convulse, knowing that she would be requiring a kiss sooner or later. The intensity of my seizures increased as she stooped and her face got closer and closer to mine. Just as she puckered up, I spotted her bus on the horizon and alerted her. It arrived just in time, as there was a good chance I would have spewed with fear if things had gone any further. We made arrangements for her to come around to my house the following Saturday when Mum and Dad were out shopping, and it was worse than the pub.

Nerves rattling, I was in danger of having an epileptic fit as Mandy arrived. I invited her upstairs into my bedroom and we sat on the bed.

'Do you like Hendrix?' I enquired, ''Cos I've got 27 albums by him.' And I proceeded to play them all.

After a while, Mandy got bored of my disc-jockeying and decided to make her move. She got off the bed, laid down on the floor, and hitched up her skirt with a look in her eye that said, 'I didn't come here to listen to your Jimi Hendrix records.'

I looked down at her long legs and even longer boots and barked out, 'My mum and dad will be home any second now, you must leave this instant, make haste, no time to tarry woman, quick, out,' or some garbled words to that effect.

After this somewhat unchivalrous outburst, I quickly marched her up to the bus stop, said my farewells and ran back home, slamming the door shut until the fear subsided. Then I went back to my bedroom, took my Hendrix album off the turntable, and danced to the music of Onan instead.

*

My first live pop music experience had been Dave Dee, Dozy, Beaky, Mick and Tich at the pantomime in Stockton, and I had sneaked under the tent at the rugby club ball once to see Juicy Lucy and the Tremeloes. But my first proper concert was The Heavy Metal Kids – who weren't heavy metal at all, and I'd never heard them, but it was a gig and a few friends were going, so I was in.

The Heavy Metal Kids turned out to be brash and loud and had a lead singer who threw himself about the stage and threatened the audience and to me seemed a bit contrived. As the show continued, the singer became even more menacing towards us and began to hurl verbal abuse.

This was an error on his part, as the Baths Hall had a balcony that hung right over the stage, and the band were directly in the firing line of any missiles that their audience might wish to launch. And launch missiles they did, starting off with balls of screwed-up paper and plastic cups, before someone moved on to the gobbing. Down it rained until the Heavy Metal Kids vanished into their dressing room. (The lead singer, by the way, was Gary Holton, who went on to play Wayne in *Auf Wiedersehen Pet*.)

In the weeks following the concert, my reservations about the quality of that particular live event were superseded by the revelation that I must be in a band. Rod Willcox already had one – the grandly named Exodus – but he was allowed to play his drums, as well as rehearse the rest of his ensemble, in the attic of his home. I needed to ditch my drums and get a guitar instead. The solution to this quandary came in the form of a small, toothy, hairy lad called Ian Wallis, who I met on a bus.

I started speaking to him because he looked like he might have a guitar, and it turned out that he did. In fact he had more than one, and he generously agreed to swap my drum kit for his old acoustic. A couple of nights later, Dad drove me and the drums round to Ian's house – a semi-detached place in the Haughton area.

The door was opened by Ian's dad, who was just as short as his son was, and wore a permanent smile. He directed me up the stairs to Ian's bedroom and I went in. I knew we would get on straight away, as his room was filled with obscure records by Neu! and Amon Düül, and if we couldn't discuss them, then we would always have the smell of sandalwood hanging heavy in the air to fall back on.

'Call me Wally,' he said. Then he picked up a Les Paul copy, plugged it in and played a blistering guitar solo, finishing off with a long, sustained vibrato note that would have put Paul Kossoff to shame. I was speechless. We swapped instruments, Wally showed me an E and C chord, and I rejoiced in the advent of a new friend and ally.

The prospect of learning actual chords on the guitar was certainly more enticing to me than any knowledge I was likely to acquire in the classroom. As the years progressed, I found I learnt more from Mum and Dad and my own reading than I ever did at school, although I did enjoy the more practical elements of history and geography.

For history, I'd spend hours doing technical drawings of German warplanes – inside and out – copied directly from *Jane's Book of Second World War Aircraft*, with the facts and figures copied painstakingly alongside in militaristically neat handwriting.

In geography, I embarked upon an ecological study of the Cocker beck, which was way over on the other side of town from where we lived. This distant waterway was chosen because the beck ran beside Cockerton Records, which supplied off-beat stuff and was therefore – in the metaphorical sense – right up my street. Once I had measured the depths of water in the beck, hauled out a jam-jar of mucky brown sludge and written 'toxicity levels' on the side of it, I felt I had done sufficient work and deserved a record from the shop as a reward.

Virgin Records had recently released a number of albums at the bargain price of 49p, and I boldly splashed out on The Faust Tapes (the work of a famously impenetrable German avant-garde outfit), Henry Cow's new disc Unrest, (uncompromisingly left-field jazz-rock) and Amon Düül II's Live in London (much the same as Faust). I loved taking risks with the buying of records, and word of mouth recommendations and tiny reviews in the *NME* would sell me a band as long as they were sufficiently off-centre.

As for the more mainstream tastes of my school-friends, most were big fans of either Yes or Genesis. There always seemed to be a split between these people – you either liked Yes or Genesis, but you couldn't like them both, even though they both made music in the same genre. The same applied to Black Sabbath and Deep Purple. 'Are you "Sabs" or "Purps"?' was an oft-heard question in the social circles I moved in. Well, I was 'Yes' and 'Sabs' – although I did like 'Purps' as well – but I also dwelt in the land of the experimental jazz turnip and had access to exotic Indian perfumes and hobbit clothes, so that made me extra special in my mind.

Even taking account of the savings I made by buying cut-price unconventional rock albums, I was still running out of money and needed to get a job quick. So off I went on my bike in search of another farm willing to employ me, and knocked on strangers' doors until I found a place in Neasham who required a boy. Sanderson's was a large market gardeners which grew tomatoes, lettuce, onions, leeks – in fact, the whole spectrum of the vegetable (and a bit of the fruit) world – and I could start on Saturday. It was great to be back at work: exams were hovering on the horizon, and I hoped tomatoes might take my mind off them.

I had only ever worked with animals before and didn't really know the difference between a lettuce and a carrot. Well, I did, but that was pretty much the full extent of my knowledge. I was keen to learn and earn at the same time, though, and I looked forward to fulfilling my Hardyesque pastoral fantasies by wearing rugged corduroy trousers held up with braces and string, a collarless shirt and a flat cap. Little did Mr Sanderson know that he had employed a worker who had already carefully planned his agrarian wardrobe.

The same carefully honed design sense applied at school, but with very different results. By this time, my uniform for academic study consisted of a pair of white split-knee loons, dyed green with Dylon, and a red and black striped tie – from another educational establishment – that I had found on the banks of the Tees and wore in preference to my own school's blue-striped neckwear. For some reason, these maverick garments seemed to slip by the eyes of the teachers. I was by this stage a tolerated rebel – a state of affairs I was exceedingly happy with.

As I left for school in the morning Mum would regularly chase me down the street waving a comb in the air. I did actually use a comb – but only for backcombing my hair into the style of a triangular thatch.

As far as careers went, my ambitions prior to CSEs and O levels were practically zero. Although I liked the idea of going to art school, neither teachers, friends nor parents seemed to think this a realistic ambition. The advice I was constantly given was to get a job 'with prospects' and thereby acquire a skill that would see me through until pensionable age. And living in the area we lived in, that meant engineering.

Trips out to visit local engineering workshops were arranged by the school so we could see what we were letting ourselves in for, and I was dispatched to the Whessoe – a titanic steel cathedral of a factory on the North Road. It was like an industrial village, with red-hot wires whipping down vast halls like scorched snakes, and crucibles filled with scalding white soups being ladled up into stone bowls by anonymous figures in blackened overalls and helmets. It all looked fiery and exciting, but could I spend the rest of my life spooning hot iron? The answer, clearly, was no.

On leaving the Whessoe, a few of us decided to go to the nearest pub and discuss the merits of the torrid steel temple we had just left steaming behind us. We entered a pub called the Star. It was a typical working man's boozer, decorated in brown, red and cream, representing the three main drinks – beer, red wine and white wine (although the last two were superfluous in this environment).

This was a place used exclusively for men to drink in, and there was something else peculiar: on every table stood a whippet. Most of them were shivering, as whippets do, and around them sat groups of men occasionally cheering and writing down notes.

The reason for this curious exhibition was that it was Friday – two days before the whippet races, which always took place on a

Sunday — and the stamina of the dogs had to be determined prior to betting on them. The animals were stood on the tabletops and pints of beer placed beneath them so they couldn't sit down.

When a dog showed signs of giving way and collapsing into the priceless pints beneath, it would be snatched away at the last moment. The last canine standing would appear to be the strongest, and therefore the one worth betting on.

This bizarre tableau didn't swing it for me, though. However else I ended up occupying myself once the imminent exams were over, I would not be plying my trade within the Whessoe's infernal realm.

CHAPTER
FIFTEEN

V.W. BEETLE

'The pair of them entwined in their passion created a terrifically hairy spectacle — like two mammoths in a battle to the death, or an explosion at a kapok factory'

As the awful day approached when exams would begin, I did, of course, make some provision for passing them. Not by revising, though.

All the time Mum and Dad thought I was hard at work in my bedroom, I was in fact sitting on the floor listening to Brian Eno's Discreet Music (my new obsession), whilst drawing my spaceship leaving earth in search of a new world ruled by hobbits with electric guitars. And if I wasn't doing that, I was laid on my bed staring at the ceiling with my hands down my pants, trying to decide what I could possibly do for a living, apart from being a prize hippy agriculturist with a penchant for old bottles.

The plan I made for passing my exams was a stroke of genius, or so I thought. My hair reached down to my nipples by now and could easily conceal pieces of paper Sellotaped to its hirsute interior — pieces of paper containing the answers to the exam questions, dates, facts and figures would be easily at my disposal, and I would therefore emerge victorious without doing a bit of revision.

The problem with this ingenious scheme was that I didn't try it out before the exams. I should have taken a leaf out of the Dam Busters' book and done a full run-through, but no, I was convinced it would work without the benefit of the tiresome process of rehearsal.

Accordingly, I entered the hall for the English exam feeling nervous but essentially confident, having made sure that none of the pieces of paper inside my hair were visible, and sat down to start the proceedings. The problem with my plan struck me instantaneously. Not only was it very, very dark inside the hairy awning, but the answer papers were situated a maximum of two inches from my eyes.

I couldn't focus on them. My deception had failed before it had even begun. I was ruined and undone and I might as well go home now, but I didn't, I sat there for the allotted time and wrote about how I thought that *The Hobbit* was much better than *The Catcher In the Rye*, but the work of Jack London was better than both of them.

Whatever the intellectual justification (or otherwise) for these observations, the problem was that none of these books nor the authors responsible for them were on the curriculum. I finished off by drawing a snake with a skull for a head up the side of the paper and was the first out of the door.

I was in better shape when it came to my art exam, and set to work straight away making the tomb of a Saxon warrior out of clay with the knight lying in repose on his casket. This ambitious project initially went roughly according to plan, but then the warrior started to look less and less like a Saxon and more and more like Shaggy from *Scooby Doo*. And the more I tried to rectify this alarming situation, the worse it became.

When I finally realised what I had actually created was a perfect representation of a bullet-headed Ken Dodd wearing wellies, despair overcame me. With less than a quarter of an hour left, I attacked the monstrosity with a mallet and beat it to a pulp, leaving a small mountain of clay with a flattened face just visible beneath, peering agonisingly out of the mound. Which was roughly how I felt, as I presented this sculptural debacle to the examiners.

From this point on, I became disillusioned with my prospects of passing even a single exam. And having decided that I would be better off down on the farm, I didn't bother turning up to the final few.

It was blisteringly hot that summer, and the cabbages had all gone rotten and begun to stink. The tomatoes needed watering constantly, and so did I – I'd turn on the sprinklers and get drenched to cool myself down, then dry out in minutes in the scorching heat. Other farm workers were collapsing, passing out in the sun and being dragged off to shady areas to recover – or even to hospital, depending on the severity of their dehydration – but I was surviving and loving the work, despite the overwhelming sultriness.

One morning, as I was tossing mouldering cabbages onto a wagon, gagging at the putrid stench, one of my teachers turned up and benignly asked me to please return to school and take my final history exam. He told me I was bright and capable and generally massaged my academic ego into going back for the final time. This I duly did, and sat my last paper honking of festering cabbages, rebelliously disregarding the set subject of twentieth-century history for a period I had more fondness for, and writing about how monks might have felt during the reformation, complete with a description and sketches of bear-baiting.

Throughout my time at school I had always felt – with the exception of Dick Welsh's art lessons – that I wasn't being taught what I wanted to learn. I had more confidence in the educational value of our family trips to castles, museums and art galleries, and didn't feel the need to have my cleverness or otherwise adjudicated by any board of examiners. The consequences of this anti-establishment attitude became apparent when I gloriously failed every exam apart from art – a failure that I saw as a triumph, although I did feel guilty about letting Mum and Dad down.

*

Away from the coalface of academic oblivion, the bulk of my evenings were now taken up with playing along to Hendrix and Fairport Convention records on the guitar. But as my technical skills were sadly lacking in this area, I soon found myself beginning to concentrate on the top four strings, playing along to the bass parts. I was mainly encouraged in this endeavour by listening to Percy Jones, who appeared on Eno's records as well as with Brand X – a motley collection of jazz-fusioneers including Phil Collins on drums.

I fiddled around for hours and reached a degree of proficiency that I felt required me to buy a proper bass guitar and think about getting a band together. In Darlington town centre, Williams' Music shop lurked seductively, and it was there that I had seen a Gibson EB3 copy, just like the one Andy Fraser from Free used. That was the instrument for me. I liked the cut of its jib. To be honest, I didn't know whether it had the right sound for me, but who cared as long as it sounded like a bass and I looked good holding it?

For a novice, the embarrassing thing about buying a guitar is that the sales assistants all sound like the axe-hero of their choice and demonstrate their prowess on the instrument you want to buy to an appreciative and rapidly swelling crowd before handing the thing over to you to continue the performance. This happened to me whilst trying to buy the EB3.

The wizard assistant played a stunning bass solo for a few minutes and then handed it expectantly over to me. I looked at it and nodded my head knowingly, fiddled with the volume and tone knobs, plucked one tremulous note and quickly thrust a bundle of notes towards him, desperate to get away from the shop and its all too knowledgeable audience.

Back at home, I realised that I needed an amp to plug into. I had heard that if you placed the guitar's machine-head against a wooden cabinet – a wardrobe in my case – sound would emerge. And so it did. So I stood there practising with the end of the guitar pressed against the wardrobe which emitted a dull but unmistakeably bassy sound.

I didn't feel as though I could go through the embarrassment of returning to the music shop, so I rang Rod Willcox to see if he had an amp and speakers I could borrow. He did, and what was more – so he claimed – it had belonged to Free's Paul Kossoff, who had apparently left it behind after a gig at Middlesbrough Town Hall.

That would do for me. The big Marshall stack duly arrived, and I set it up in my bedroom. All the pieces of the jigsaw were now in place. All that remained was for me to become a bass hero, find a band and make my astonishing debut to tremendous applause in a very short time.

*

Rising at 6am every morning and heading off on my bike to the farm, which was about six miles away, I would pass dozens of men, all cycling to work, like me, and almost all of them whistling the shrill, trilling tunes that seemed to have no beginning or end and only the most negligible melody. All of them would say, 'Good morning'. This, along with the balmy weather, would put me in a beautiful mood for the day.

In recent times, the whistling cyclist seems to have become sadly extinct. In fact, even street whistlers are a dying breed. But I remain to this day an avid practitioner of this bygone art. And while this is occasionally commented on as being something of an oddity, I believe it is only natural for those who don't carry a Walkman or an iPod^{TM} – as I don't – to want to create their own music. Anyway, those boys could whistle to a higher pitch and louder than anyone I have heard since – you could hear them from miles away, their high vibratos quivering ecstatically through the morning air.

I soon became the head boy at the farm, and, after telling them that I was a highly skilled tractor driver, found myself rapidly promoted to ploughing duties. What I didn't tell them, was that I wasn't very good at changing gears and generally felt happier just leaving it in first. I was also prone to misjudging gate widths and pulling down fencing.

The tractor I drove was much nicer than the one I had previously used, and after being shown the basics I was told to take it down to a field by the river ready for furrowing. I started her up, slipped her into gear and reversed into a pig pen, taking out an entire length of wall. Thankfully there were no pigs in it, but I had razed it to the ground and had to come clean. My attempts at rebuilding it were pitiful; there was no way I could cover my tracks.

Mr Sanderson was a nice, kind man and forgave me, saying that the pen was going to come down anyway so there was no harm done there. The harm came later, when I started ploughing. The way to plough a field is to find a point of reference at the other end of the waiting expanse and aim your tractor at it, keeping your line as straight as possible so you're left with a lovely straight groove. This is vital, because on your way back you are going to stick your wheel in this groove and use it as a guide furrow for a nicely geometrical overall effect.

It was a lovely hot day as I started my guide furrow, and I still had the arcane melodies of the cycling whistlers flitting around in my head. At some point on my journey from one end of the field to the other I must have dropped off for a moment, but I wasn't going to hit anything and it was only for a second, so no harm done. It was a fairly large field of about twenty acres and I spent the morning happily ploughing away. It was only when I stopped for lunch that I saw the awful results of my momentary snooze.

Following my guide furrow, I had ploughed half the field with a giant 'U' bend in the middle. I had thus created a 'joke' field. Farmers would travel from miles around to laugh at my comedy enclosure. They would lean on the fence and giggle at the funny furrows and roar at the riotous, rib-tickling ruts. I was taken off ploughing duties with immediate effect, and that was the last time I ever drove a tractor.

As I sat silently in the van on the way back to the farm, the shame leaking from my scarlet chops in little sweaty beads, there was a monumental explosion in the back, and the vehicle swerved all over the road. 'What in heaven's name was that?' I exclaimed. Or words to that effect, only rendered almost entirely in expletives.

'That, Mr Plough King, was a crow-scarer,' replied Mr Sanderson. 'It just went off by accident.' For anyone who doesn't know what a crow-scarer is, well, it's a device that forces air through a cylinder to keep ravening corvines away from the fields, and it sounds like ten 12-bore shotguns going off at the same time. In fact, it sounds like an anti-aircraft gun. And when it goes off in the confined space of a tiny Vauxhall Viva van, it sounds more like a nuclear device in a cake tin. All the next week my hearing was accompanied by a high-pitched ringing.

*

Looking through the papers for a less dangerous form of employment, I noticed that there was an opening for someone to look after the police horses at Aykley Heads police training school. This fitted in neatly with my love of animals and farming, and also seemed in accord with the universally accepted need for a 'good, solid job with prospects'. So I applied forthwith and was invited shortly after to attend an interview and test.

I turned up at Aykley Heads along with a group of people the same age as me, who immediately began a relentless taunting session directed at me and my glorious hair, which they for some reason found hilarious. They all favoured a hairstyle blow-dried into the shape of a bell, and held in place with gallons of hairspray lest it might be shifted by a stray gust of wind and, God forbid, look faintly human. I found their style amusing – if slightly frightening – in its turn, but having been raised to be polite, I decided to forego pointing this out.

A further shock awaited me inside the police training school. In order to look after the horses, it turned out that I would have to become a policeman. I hadn't bargained for that, and I had no intention of joining the fuzz, so I told them at the interview that they could stick their job up their arses. No I didn't, but I did imagine that I did during the interview and I believe it was obvious that I was clearly stifling laughter as they told me of the extremely important job at hand.

I decided to stick around and do the written test just for fun, and what a test it was. One of the questions was 'Spot the odd man out: (a) Hammer (b) Chisel (c) Squirrel', and there were people there who got it wrong. I have a great admiration for our police force and the work they do, but they don't half attract a lot of morons to their job interviews.

So it was back to the farm for the time being. Returning home from work at 5.30pm each day, I would swiftly have my tea and get back on my bike to ride over to the other side of town to see a girl I had met and found very pleasant company.

Her name was Jill, and after I had called at her house we would walk down by the river and push each other while laughing and talking about music. We had reasonably similar tastes in bands and she was very pretty, so I thought this an excellent coupling. On these temperate summer evenings we watched the swallows and flies buzzing over the idle river whilst I pushed her gently onto the bank and we giggled, then she'd try to get up and I'd push her back down again.

Each night the same thing happened. I should have known that a girl wants more from a relationship than a series of shoves and nudges, at least, not the sort I was offering anyway. Perhaps I should have varied my shoving technique when I had decked her onto the riverbank, instead of (as was my regular custom) running away while inviting her to try and find me as I crouched behind a hawthorn tree.

I knew it couldn't last. My shyness around females was all too apparent once again, but I thought kissing her would be an impropriety, so the moment of doom came briskly.

One sunny evening, I arrived at Jill's house and knocked on the door as I always did, but there was no reply. Peering through the letterbox, I saw movement.

It was her sister, who looked medieval in her approach – wearing a long purple velvet gown and long, long black hair. She was lying down on the floor, halfway into the hall, her bottom half obscured within the sitting room. And rolling around on top of her was a person with more hair than I had ever seen: a giant triangle of wavy hair at least three feet across and the same in length. This was her boyfriend, and the pair of them entwined in their passion created a terrifically hairy spectacle – like two mammoths in a battle to the death, or an explosion at a kapok factory.

I was – understandably – riveted by the scene, but quickly realised that I was becoming a peeping Tom, and retreated to the garden gate trying to decide what would be a reasonable length of time to wait before I knocked again. How long did they require for their tumble? I gave them a full minute, and then knocked again.

This time, the door was answered by Jill's dishevelled and baroque-looking sister.

'Is Jill in?' I enquired, and back came the answer – already half expected, but nevertheless, it hit me like a gunshot. 'She's in her bedroom with her new boyfriend.'

I thought I was her new boyfriend, so who was this fellow, and what was he doing in her bedroom?

Fire and jealousy ripped through me, and I considered barging past Jill's sister, tearing up the stairs, and confronting this amorous intruder – slapping him with my slimline cycling gloves and challenging him to a duel. Perhaps a contest as to who could name the most bands or singers beginning with Z.

ZZ Top, Zappa, yes, he might get them, but would he get Warren Zevon or Joe Zawinul from Weather Report (admittedly a saxophonist, not a singer, but if I could pronounce his name with sufficient confidence, there was a good chance my deception might go undetected)? I would beat him easily, and then Jill would throw him out and fall at my feet, asking me to push her again, the way I used to. But, of course, I didn't.

'OK,' I said instead. 'Bye.'

And away I rode with salty tears blurring my vision, cursing her and myself and feeling utterly heartbroken. My vision was so impaired by watery grief that I smashed into the back of a parked Volkswagen Beetle. I stopped to inspect any damage and then checked out the design of the Beetle. It looked really cool in its bright yellow livery. I would get one of those when I learned how to drive.

Well done to Volkswagen for coming up with such a cute design. My heartbreak over, thanks to the yellow Beetle, I cycled home with the intention of starting my band immediately. Then loads of girls would be queuing up to get pushed over by me.

*

I called my friend Wally and suggested we might get together and form a band. He had my old drum kit and guitar, and I had my bass. All we needed was another group member and we would be away. And so it was that one morning we set up in the sitting room of his friend Robin Powton's house, with Wally on drums, Robin on guitar, and me on bass.

We posed for a while, placing mirrors strategically around the room so we could see ourselves to make sure we were looking sufficiently mean and sultry. Guitarists at the time had an abundance of possible facial expressions to fall back on, like Hendrix's tongue-quivering surprised look, or Paul Kossoff's enormously wide-mouthed countenance – an expression that suggested he was being anally interfered with by a peppered mutton. The most varied collection of pained faces was showcased by Robin Trower, whose grotesque facial contortions sent concertgoers fleeing from his gigs, either to seek psychiatric help, or return with a rifle, depending on their strength of character.

Robin Powton was rather less extravagant and opted for a calm, collected approach with one leg up on a box – like John Williams or some other classical guitarist. The worry was that at the end of a song he might turn to the rest of us and say, 'And rest', but we never got to the end of a song so this concern proved groundless.

Wally was a highly skilled guitarist and presumably in that guise had a wide range of impressive facial twists, but he was playing the drums, and went for the muppet/Cousin It style, with hair down over face, emerging only when a gulp of air was required and then retreating back behind the hairy curtain. There may have been several grimaces being practised behind that veil, but we were never to witness them.

As a rule, bass-players were notoriously dull in their approach. Bill Wyman of the Rolling Stones and The Who's John Entwhistle – a.k.a. the Ox – being typically motionless. There were exceptions. Chris Squire from Yes had an interesting raised leg movement that made him appear flatulent and keen to release his gases. And I liked Andy Fraser's back and forth rocking motion. But I ultimately settled on a style that suggested I had seen something interesting on the horizon over to my left.

This gave me the appearance of being fully in charge of my instrument while having a coolness that hinted I would rather be doing something else. I added a daring variation to this stance by occasionally putting a stop to the horizon-gazing and suddenly becoming interested in ornaments placed around the room instead.

When we were on stage, these ornaments would be replaced by people whom I could cast a glance at and either cockily dismiss or reward with an impish, mischievous smile. This, combined with an occasional spasm sending me bent over backwards, satisfied me enough to begin to rock. And did we rock? A bit, yes.

We decided that our musical style should emulate Hawkwind, as they were powerful enough to sound heroic and yet rarely played more than three chords, leaving us plenty of creative energy to concentrate on our stances. We began playing a powerhouse version of 'Master of the Universe' at about 11 o'clock, and eventually ground to a halt at 4.30pm, by which time we had collected a fan club outside Robin's house.

Some local Bay City Rollers fans of approximately fourteen years of age and wearing the full Rollers costumes had heard our din and began to gather outside, waving their tartan scarves and howling 'Woody!' and 'Derek Longmuir!' at us. I reciprocated by exaggerating my movements, giving them nods and winks and generally entertaining them whilst retaining an air of coolness. This was my first audience and I liked it. Yes, it was a rock star's life for me.

But rock stars lived by night, and I still needed a day job. So I began attending interviews at various factories around the area. One of these was a place that made brake regulators in Newton Aycliffe. SAB, or – to give it its full title – something Swedish like Svensk Automastik Bromsregulator, was a large new building on a large new industrial estate.

I arrived there on the bus for my interview wearing new loons, a new mustard cheesecloth shirt and a bottle-green velvet jacket – looking more like I should be attending an interview for Radio Caroline than one at a major engineering works.

I did well, though, telling them that I would like to end up working in the technical drawing department (the nearest I was going to get to doing any artwork). And, following the interview, the manager Mr Edmunssen offered me an apprenticeship that would last five years.

I didn't know whether I was happy or sad. The thought of working there every day instead of painting or practising at being a rock star daunted me considerably. But Mammon won out. The thought of piles of money rising gradually over the years greatly appealed. I could buy better bass guitars and amps, more records and clothes and that prospect made me very happy. So happy that

I went straight down to Guru and bought a great big stinking Afghan coat and enough patchouli oil to stun an elephant.

CHAPTER
SIXTEEN

THE
TRUSS

"When you're a skilled man like me", he said, "you'll be able to make one of these"

A series of seismic shifts were about to take place in my musical and social outlook. The epicentre of these adolescent earthquakes was – perhaps inevitably – a public house. There were plenty of pubs in Darlington that could qualify as meeting places for young novice drinkers such as myself, but the one which seemed to harbour the most like-minded people was the Green Dragon on Posthouse Wynd.

The main bar was a long thin room, and at the very end of it sat the cream of the hairies: a dense and seemingly impenetrable agglomeration of denim, leather, Indian-wear, beads and hair, all crammed into a small space and secretly discussing mysterious subjects like how to achieve maximum width of hair and the recipes for spicy, redolent fragrances known only to ancient sages from the East. Or at least that's what I suspected.

In reality, they were probably talking about their work at the paper-bag factory or the wool cleaners, or what time they reckoned the shellfish man would be round with his little pots of winkles. But to me they were strangely mythical, romantic characters who were only a few years older than me yet could have come from a distant age and land. And I duly wormed my way in with them – boldly side-stepping the seating hierarchy and taking my place right in their midst.

Having seated myself at the helm of the Green Dragon, I began to meet new friends and told them of my band and how with one unexpectedly public sitting-room rehearsal and barely one song to our name, I was thinking of breaking off and doing my own thing. I was, after all, a seasoned bassist with a gig under my belt, and so I was introduced to Michael Jackson, a drummer without a band and as eager as me to get a serious progressive rock outfit together.

We both liked King Crimson and Yes and decided to head off in that direction, but we two members would not be sufficient, and after following a few leads picked up amid the heady aromas of the Green Dragon, we met with a lad slightly younger than us and in a similar situation. Trevor Gilligan was a young guitar genius and Peter Frampton lookalike. There were two bonuses to start off with, and the third was that his dad owned a carpentry business and had a large workshop which we could rehearse in at immense volume.

We met at the workshop that week with our instruments and jammed for hours; Trev clearly taking the lead with his huge array of effects pedals, creating sounds I had never heard before. He had a pretty good singing voice as well, even though he sounded like Peter Frampton. His only downfall was that he couldn't ever remember the words to any songs and compensated by filling in the gaps with lyrics of his own which he made up on the spot. These were excruciatingly dire – usually something like 'And she looked like a woman and she drove a car/And she wore perfume and she would go far.'

Mike was a drummer from the Keith Moon wildman-of-rock school, but with aspirations to becoming a Bill Bruford-style cultured percussion master, which he might possibly have been able to pull off, had it not been for the fact that as soon as excitement took a grip he'd go off into one of his uninhibited Moony moments and start thrashing his kit around like a dervish. Still, we gelled pretty well, and our mighty three-piece was well and truly born. All we needed now was a name, so off we went to the Dragon to celebrate and come up with one.

Trev's ideas in this department were predictably akin to his song lyrics. He offered up suggestions such as The Killer Boys and Witch Woman. The latter led to our first inter-band bickering session as we protested that it sounded like a woman's magazine. Mike's nomenclatural notions were slightly more in keeping with how the band might actually sound, but still seemed a bit too spacey – featuring as they did various combinations of Xs and random groups of numbers. After X156 had been dismissed, he came up with some clearly unacceptable and filthy names based on expletives and bodily functions.

All my names were based on wildlife and especially creatures that I thought had amusing names, like Finch, Stoat and Partridge. After a long and heated debate we opened it up to friends in the pub to pick the best of our suggestions. One of my names won out and from that night on we were to be called Trout.

*

In my first year at SAB, I was set to work learning all aspects of my new trade. This entailed signing on at the glamorously named

South West Durham Training Centre, with a day release to the similarly exotic-sounding Darlington Technical College. Starting at the training centre was like starting at school again, only with more testosterone gusting about.

On the first day, chests were puffed out to the maximum and jaws jutted, Mussolini-style. It was like a blue-collar mafia convention and I felt I didn't really fit in, so I stood back and watched the parade bluster by, leaning campily on a short bed lathe.

They weren't all muscle-flexing brutes, though. In fact, there were plenty of boys there who kept their virility concealed, and some who didn't care whether it was displayed or not. I, of course, sat firmly with the latter. The correctness of this decision was confirmed by the macho crowd who immediately dubbed me 'Mary' Moir – a title that I presume referred to my hair and clothes, and one that was intended to cause offence, but actually I quite liked it. And when a cry of, 'Ow, Mary!' was let loose across the workshop, I would turn and face the caller with a smile.

I had friends at the training centre too, of course. My schoolmate Steve Parry was there, training for his apprenticeship at Torringtons, another factory nearby. There was also Graham Garney, a new friend who worked at SAB, and we all got along nicely – milling and turning and drilling and welding, and generally doing all the things you do in a factory.

On Tuesdays, I went to Darlington Technical College on day-release for instruction in engineering's scientific and technological aspects. We were taught by Mr Brown who was an old-school lecturer with bottle-bottom glasses that made his eyes appear to be somewhere in the region of six miles away. He also had a hernia. This we knew because he wore a truss – a huge pouch about five inches round that was visible beneath his white lab coat.

He would rest it on the edge of the table whilst he was talking, and sometimes he scraped it along the length of the table edge – perhaps relieving an itch, or maybe he just liked the feel of it. Whatever the reason, I was transfixed. And whilst Mr Brown told us of torque stresses and molecular division, all I could think of was the stresses he was enduring within his giant truss, as he dragged and tapped it on the table before me.

The Tech' was situated directly next door to the Sixth Form College. This latter establishment appeared to house people to whom I would be able to relate with more ease.

And so, after I had finished my session examining Mr Brown's truss, I crept up into the sixth-form common room and hung about like an impostor, which is exactly what I was: a snake in the grass, a lurker, a shadowy figure on the periphery of people's conversations. I later discovered that I appeared mysterious, if not downright sinister, with my unrestrained hair and voluminous trenchcoat. But I was simply there seeking friends with similar likes, and before long I would find them.

Fridays were spent doing bits and pieces at SAB – helping out here and there, and meeting the other workers, some of whom had been affected by years of engineering and had perhaps come into contact with mercurial elements, certainly something that causes a faint corrosion of the mind. There was a chap called Mick the Miller – his name was Mick and he operated a milling machine, so no one felt it necessary to come up with a more original nickname.

Anyway, Mick was a small, slightly wizened man about 55 years old, and the proud owner of an enormous Hampton, yard, prong or whatever you wish to call it. No words could do this giant justice, and with new boys like myself in the building, he was eager to present his party piece.

I was called over to Mick's machine, where he had unleashed his monster and laid it on a rag on the machine-bed (which he'd previously wound down to groin level), before covering this awesome protuberance with another rag. 'When you're a skilled man like me,' he said, 'you'll be able to make one of these'. And then he whipped away the rag to reveal the donkey-rigging.

At first I thought it was a rolling pin and was less than impressed at his skills. Then it struck me (not literally – though if it had, it would certainly have knocked me out), and I let loose an ear-splitting roar, which combined approval, fear and disgust in one mighty bellow. Apparently satisfied with this reaction, he hauled the beast back into his trousers – like a lifeboat returning to its house – ready for the next victim.

The next victim was always Mary, the tea lady, who came round on regular circuits delivering brews. As she approached Mick, the machine-bed was wound down and Mick heaved his Master John Goodfellow out of his capacious slacks and laid it out for her perusal, just as he had done with me. At this juncture, Mary would scream and run off in shock and terror. This happened two or three times a day, so either Mary had the memory of a goldfish, or she enjoyed her visits to Mick's machine and the fuss and pantomime that surrounded it. I suspect the latter.

Most of the men were either called Mick or George (or sometimes 'Geordie', as colloquialism decreed). There were a few exceptions, though. Jack Ghundoo was one – a 60-year-old Indian, who separated himself from the rest of the workers and worked like a Trojan.

He was the first Asian I had ever met and I found him intriguing to talk to. He started off in the merchant navy – sailing from India to England – and told me of his adventures on the high seas. He once removed his turban and showed me his hair which fell to his knees, a hirsute vista which – needless to say, given my own ambitions in this area – impressed me immensely.

Another character was Ray, who worked in the stores. It was Ray who would end up giving me a lift into work each day in his Austin A30 – dropping me off at the training centre or taking me directly into the factory. Ray was a plain-looking man with tales of sexual adventure that would make a nymph of darkness blush. These were clearly all fictional, but that only intensified the delight with which he recounted them.

The priapic sagas would begin as soon as I got in the car. He had shacked up with gangs of leopardskin-leotarded student nurses and been used by them as their plaything. He had been interfered with by scantily clad maids in hotel rooms, and – most incredibly – by the servant girls of a visiting Danish royal.

All his stories could've – and most probably already had – appeared in a cheap porno movie, but I got them on a daily basis nonetheless. Those tall tales that weren't about his own earthy exploits would generally feature low characters who were indiscreet with flocks of sheep in the high-lying rural communities in Durham where Ray was raised. I was forever trying to change the subject, and very often sat squirming in my seat.

When Ray grew tired of his coarse boasts, his conversation would turn to some new scheme he was developing to get out of the rat race and make enormous amounts of money. Most of these proposals he couldn't tell me about, as they were veiled in secrecy, but one he couldn't help but share with me involved his plan to import millions of shoes from the Middle East, as he had heard rumours that footwear was going cheap there.

He was going to stash them all in a warehouse in Ashington and throw out all the ones with curly toes, or maybe keep them and sell them on to theatrical agents or circuses. He had slept with a theatrical agent once, and she would be able to help him out. I felt sorry for Ray. His life wasn't what he wanted it to be, and so he filled up the empty space with fantasies and doomed plans. I wasn't going to allow this to happen to me.

*

Weeks of rehearsals in Trev Gilligan's dad's woodwork shop had left Trout with the beginnings of a repertoire – a collection of songs that reflected our varying musical inclinations. Well, mainly mine and Trev's, as Mike was quite happy to go along with whatever he was asked to drum to, although he tended to lean more in my direction if pressed. Trev liked straightforward pop/rock songs, and so we played 'Five Years' by David Bowie, something from Queen's Sheer Heart Attack, UFO's 'Doctor Doctor', and Trev's own composition, 'The Lion, the Witch and the Wardrobe'.

Presumably this must have been a favourite book from his youth. Sadly, as with all of Trev's songs, the music and the playing were great but the words were all wrong. We all know what *The Lion, the Witch and the Wardrobe* is about, so how did this line happen?

'Because the Lion the Witch and the Wardrobe is coming on strong'.

Not only is the grammar upsetting, but the thought of a wardrobe 'coming on' to anyone creates an intensely troubling image. I didn't care, though. I never even noticed, and neither did anyone else. And even if they did, it still didn't matter. If Yes could get away with singing about 'nailing sad preachers against coloured doors of time' then we were all right with a lascivious wardrobe. But it was when Trev got around to singing the lyrics to my songs that I took umbrage.

I had recently read *The Lord of the Rings* and become quite unnervingly obsessed by it. My songs reflected this growing fascination. One was a complicated 3/4, 4/4, 3/29 composition about the Black Riders, the monstrous servants of Sauron, mounted on black fiery-eyed steeds. I wrote the powerful, doom-laden music and handed over the lyric-writing to Trev, telling him what the song was about.

The outcome was a song about the Black Riders, which was just what I'd hoped for. The only problem came when Trev added the line: 'They're gonna make love to you', and backed up this alarming threat with proud boasts of the supernatural horsemen's ability to 'Keep goin' all night long'.

Trevor was an excellent guitarist, but his lyrical prowess left a lot to be desired. And mine wasn't much better. I wrote a song called 'Let's Eat Out Tonight', which told the story of a husband and wife who had discovered that the pantry was empty and therefore decided to dine out. And that was about it. I took care of the vocals on this song, and sang in my best Paul Rodgers impersonator's voice.

A rasping, bluesy singer suggesting a meal in a restaurant was not exactly the stuff of rock'n'roll greatness, but who cared? We looked good, and the poses were all there. We were ready to 'Let the Good Times Roll' (which, incidentally, was the other song I took lead vocals on).

Our first gig was at the woodwork shop in front of a selected audience of friends from the Green Dragon. Wally, Tally and Noggy were there, along with some new friends from the sixth-form common room. Amongst them was Geoff Dent, who was another *Lord of the Rings* obsessive and had the longest hair of any boy in Darlington: a straight flat length of blond strands falling down to his waist, the effect rounded off with a pair of National Health specs.

Geoff brought some girls along with him, and with other friends of friends in tow, we ended up with an audience of about 25 – all seated on the floor amongst the sawdust, tugging on tins of lager, puffing Regals and watching and listening to us rock through our first live performance.

After a while, their spirits loosened by beer, they slowly – one by one – rose from their recumbent positions and began to sway self-consciously in time with the music. This was easy if it was one of Trev's songs, but pretty much impossible if I had been left in charge of the timings. But sway they did, and after 45 minutes we left the 'stage' to hearty applause.

We celebrated our triumphant debut in the Green Dragon – basking in glory as we planned where to play our second gig. Next time, we vowed to test our mettle in front of an actual paying audience of non-sycophantic music lovers. But meanwhile, there were advantages to playing for a friendly crowd.

One of the girls who had been present at the gig was an attractive, slim, curly-haired girl called Teri, to whom I off-handedly suggested that it might be a good idea if she were to become my girlfriend – an offer which she accepted. I went home that night with self-esteem burgeoning. I was now in a top band, and I had a girl on my arm to boot.

CHAPTER SEVENTEEN

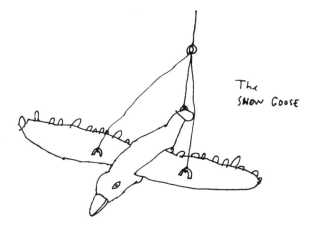

The
SNOW GOOSE

'Our evenings were spent huddled in a tight group in a corner of the Dragon, entertaining ourselves with amusing words, random scenarios and various diversions that revolved around our own peculiar and insular world'

T rout were not the only band in town. Looming large amongst the competition were Rod Willcox's Exodus, who had recently changed their name to Iroqouo and featured a guitarist called Speedy Jolliff who wore a top hat with 'Speed' written on it. They played Genesis-style prog-rock with great expertise and were probably the main threat to our rock sovereignty. Then there was the Thin Lizzy-esque Jailbait, and a seven-foot maverick called Mick Hall who had a Zappa-style outfit called Stinkfoot.

All the main bands in Darlington played at the Bowes wine cellar – a tiny underground cavern on Skinnergate – and that seemed to be the venue for us. I had seen a couple of bands play down there (one of them being The Beautiful Losers, with a young Chris Rea on guitar) and we felt we could handle it, so a date was secured. We had to make sure we could pull it off, so rehearsals were increased to achieve maximum professional capability.

Trevor's dad's woodwork shop was an old coaching stables and had a reputation for being haunted. We did occasionally hear strange unexplained sounds coming from distant corners of the building. In fact, these creaks and knocks were commonplace, and we ended up simply ignoring them.

One night, whilst taking a break in between songs, we heard footsteps coming up the stairs towards where we were rehearsing. Trev assumed it was his dad and called out. Response came there none, and further investigation revealed that there was no one in the building apart from us. This chilling episode put an end to our evening's practice and we went home feeling decidedly uncomfortable, Trev slightly less so, as he said he'd experienced such sounds before.

A week later, we were pounding away at our instruments as usual when, once again, the knocks and bangs began. We stopped playing and listened in silence, shivers running not just down our spines as normal shivers do, but pretty much all over us. We called out, and again, no reply came. Then, just as we were about to start playing again, a ten-foot plank that was sitting on a workbench in front of us flew up into the air and landed on the floor.

We dropped our instruments and fled down the stairs and out into the alley outside. Mike and Trev stood peering back into the workshop through one of the small windows in the door, whilst I stood about fifteen feet behind them. From this vantage point, I was able to observe a three-foot high, egg-shaped mist, hovering two feet above the ground, which passed quite clearly through them, out into the middle of the alley and then vanished.

Surprisingly calmly, I said, 'Did you see that? A ghost just went straight through you.' They panicked, jumping up and down, nervously laughing and brushing nonexistent ectoplasm from their clothing.

Someone had to go back inside to turn off the amps, but who? We decided to all go together, ran in and out as quickly as possible, and then went off to the Dragon to tell people of our supernatural evening, where our chilling account was mercilessly derided, largely because people could not believe how matter-of-fact we were being.

We had just encountered an unearthly spectre. A shadowy phantom had recently passed straight through two people. And we felt perfectly nonchalant about it. We should have been shaking with fear, weeping and tearing out our hair, but instead we calmly related our story to an audience of deaf ears.

This experience should act as a caution to anyone who stumbles across a passing ghoul, or indeed any unnatural phenomenon – be it a globe-headed alien, a swamp beast or even a speaking mouse. If you want people to believe your story, act like you're terrified, act like you may never recover from this trauma. In fact, act as if you've seen a ghost.

*

Hanging around in the sixth-form common room and at the Green Dragon, I made friends with a new group of people. We were to become an inseparable and curious gang. First, there was John Irvine, or 'The Doctor', or 'Doc' as he was also known, for what reasons I don't know (and neither, I think, did he). Although he was seen wearing a white lab-coat on various occasions and had a penchant for peculiar science, especially in music. Then came

Graham Bristow, who was also known as 'Herbert', on account of his pimpled face as a youth. These wens had vanished by now, but the nickname remained. Then there was Robert Colebrook, who didn't have a nickname as yet, but this omission was soon to be rectified. And along with the long-haired Geoff Dent, the five of us became a gang whose doctrine was, to all intents and purposes, 'Humour at all costs'.

I first became good friends with John (Doc), who was originally a mate of Wally's, when I went round to his house to borrow a fuzz-pedal. His bedroom wall was adorned with drawings and scribbling he had done featuring characters he had invented, such as 'Jack Pelt', who it seemed was some kind of astronaut. Then there was 'Scruffy Woolard', and various diagrams of dogs on hang-gliders, as well as the obligatory Pink Floyd poster of the pyramid which was Sellotaped to many a bedroom wall in this period.

He also had a tape recorder like me, and a WEM Copycat – a kind of crude, early echo machine in which he and his brother Richard had stretched the tape to make the delay on the echo fabulously long. These tape loops were recorded with backing from a red Woolworth's chord organ, and rhythm from some biscuit tins. John would later record and operate the tapes for the *Big Night Out*, but this was where it all began.

I had initially been impressed by John when I saw him receiving a random haircut from a girl in the Green Dragon. He seemingly had very little consideration for convention as far as hairstyling went, and requested that she slice off one side of his shoulder-length hair in a rudimentary style, leaving the other side long. Everyone found this hilarious, and John went along with the 'joke' hairdo by acting sincere and thankful.

He had also been dining from the same musical bowl as me, and particularly liked Todd Rundgren, Van Der Graf Generator, Tangerine Dream and Amon Düül II. In fact, he once sent his mum, who was a Methodist minister, off to buy Phallus Dei by Amon Düül II.

She returned with the album and said to John, 'Do you know what this title means?'

'No,' replied John in all innocence.

'It means "God's Penis" in Latin,' she explained – plainly not best pleased. But I was when he told me. As well as liking the same obscure bands, we shared a penchant for odd sketches and a similar outlook on life, so an affiliation was inevitable, and we promised to invent some music together at some later stage.

Our evenings were spent huddled in a tight group in a corner of the Dragon, entertaining ourselves with amusing words, random scenarios and various diversions that revolved around our own peculiar and insular world. And when we weren't making our own fun, we were attending rock concerts.

Amongst the most memorable of these was Camel at Middlesbrough Town Hall. Camel were a mostly instrumental prog-rock group built around Pete Barden's keyboard wizardry, who had enjoyed recent success with the release of their concept album, The Snow Goose, based on the children's story by Paul Gallico.

This may have been the inspiration for Trout's similarly ground-breaking composition 'The Lion, the Witch and the Wardrobe', but that's no excuse for anyone to base any music on children's stories, let alone a double LP and a national tour. But The Snow Goose was and remains a great album, and I sat in the balcony enjoying every minute of the performance, an occasion marred only by the slide-show behind the band, which showed images of wildfowl in various locations, feeding, nesting and paddling about.

From where I was sitting, the sound of the slides shifting in and out of the projector was almost louder than the group and I found this highly amusing – nudging my companions into giggles that turned into guffaws. And then the cherry on the cake appeared. From behind us, for the final crescendo of the piece, came a six-foot wing-spanned Snow Goose hanging from a wire and being manually dragged over the heads of the audience by what one can only presume to have been a very tired roadie.

The bird flew over us in fits and starts, like someone pulling out washing on a line. It had clearly seen a bit of action. There were places where the feathers had fallen off and chicken wire was clearly visible. This caused us to erupt in a veritable volcano of laughter – I hope that Camel didn't hear us from the stage. If they did, then I can only apologise and say that it will never happen again.

My future partner in amusement, Bob Mortimer, was also at this legendary concert and, although we didn't know each other then, we have since been united in the memory of 'the Goose'. And the spirit of that noble bird might even be said to live on in *Shooting Stars*' 'Dove from above'.

Another notable gig at Middlesbrough Town Hall was Judas Priest. First of all, we saw singer Rob Halford in a pub before the show. He strutted his way through the bar in his studded leathers and leather-peaked cap, carrying a walking cane. Rob later stunned the very heterosexual world of heavy metal by announcing that he was gay.

Seeing him parade through the pub in this costume, he appeared to us nothing but testosterone-stinkingly manly, and not in the slightest bit gay. And I should know, as I was forever being pestered by men winking in my direction or trying to rub up against me.

In fact, the week before the Judas Priest gig, I had been to see Be Bop Deluxe at the Mayfair in Newcastle and found myself consistently bedevilled by a stevedore – well, that's certainly what he looked like, or maybe some kind of seafarer with a very ruddy complexion.

However he made his living, he clearly took a fancy to me, and wherever I went, he was there beside me with a lopsided grin and an offer of a pint. I don't know why, but it was always me who was singled out for this kind of attention – presumably on account of my girlish good looks. But I was already accustomed to provoking diverse reactions with my sartorial flamboyance.

At school there was a boy who, whenever he passed me in the corridor, would punch me squarely in the face, or wherever was convenient. His attacks were entirely unjustified – it was probably my appearance that offended him. The fact that he was a soul boy and I was a hippy upset him so much that he insisted on asserting his authority by assaulting me whenever he had the opportunity.

This didn't particularly bother me; it was merely a faint inconvenience – I could withstand the punches, and there was no mental torture because I didn't know him. In fact, I never knew his name. He was always referred to by me as 'Ron Don the big Mong'. His attacks came silently; there was no insult or humiliating name-calling or explanation, just a thump and he was gone. This continued even after I left school, until I eventually confronted him.

When I politely asked him why he had so regularly struck me over the years, he replied, 'Because I don't like you.' At this point, everything became clear. If there was someone or something he didn't like the look of, he punched it. The strange thing was, after we'd had this conversation, he asked if he could be my friend.

Anyway, back to the Priest gig. Once inside, myself and Wally took a position right up front by the PA system. As the night drew on, so the sweat increased, and we took off our denim jackets and, for safety, jammed them in the bass bins at the bottom of the PA. This, of course, is a very foolish thing to do, as any roadie will tell you. But we weren't roadies, so we didn't know. And here's what happened as a result of our ignorance.

A bass bin needs air to circulate around the cones in order to keep it cool – otherwise it will eventually explode, a bit like a cooling system in a car engine. At first there was an acrid stink that we could only put down to the smell of Rob Halford's leather trousers rubbing together. Then came smoke, and finally flames: our jackets had caught fire.

We removed them and got away without burning down the building, although that was not the only mistake I made that evening. In the course of retrieving the smouldering garments, I stuck my head right inside the bass bin and spent the following week with a high-pitched ringing in my ears almost as bad as the one I got from the crow-scarer.

Mike and I also camped overnight at the Durham Dome festival. This was a small regional rock extravaganza, held on the banks of the Wear, in the shadow of Durham Cathedral. The night before the scheduled entertainment, we camped beside the stage. There was only one other tent apart from ours, and this contained some girls who occasionally made whooping sounds. So we whooped back, and eventually progressed from this Neanderthal mating ritual to make contact using modern-day language.

They came over to our encampment, sat around the fire, and we offered them a tin of beer. Mike clearly got on well with one of the girls and began to canoodle with her on the periphery of the camp. Her friend disappeared primly back into their tent leaving me with the third girl, who was quite a hefty individual. I chivalrously offered her a digestive biscuit and another tin of beer which she gratefully accepted, and she then proceeded to demolish the entire packet, and the rest of the beer, and whatever other consumables we had lying around.

When her mouth wasn't filled with our provisions, she looked at me tenderly through spatterings of beans, cheese and biscuit crumbs and said, 'You're nice, you, aren't you.' This was, I presumed, a statement and not a question.

And I had no response other than a nervous, 'Ha Ha, erm, I don't know, am I?'

She duly confirmed her diagnosis: 'Yes, you are,' with a look in her eye which suggested this might be the prelude to her making a lustful lunge in my direction. I was becoming more and more frightened, and attempted to call an end to the evening by yawning and announcing that I was getting into my sleeping bag.

This I did, and it was at this moment that she made her final, desperate bid for my affection, by trying to wedge herself into the bag with me. She must have weighed at least sixteen stone, and as she forced her way into my cocoon, I was jammed in, my arms pinned to my sides with no means of escape. I panicked and began to scream for help.

Mike came running to my rescue, but his commendable sense of urgency soon gave way to fits of uncontrollable laughter. This, fortunately, acted as the perfect deterrent. The girl began to haul her immense and legitimately aggrieved bulk out of my accommodation and – prior to returning to her own – announced, 'Actually, you're not nice, are you,' which, again, I took as a statement and wearily agreed with.

*

In the meantime, my days at the South West Durham Training Centre had come to an end. I had learnt the skills required to become an engineer, and left with a collection of objects that I had made over the year – a vice, a poker, various measuring jugs and other assorted engineering artefacts, all carried away in a bespoke toolbox made from sheet steel with my very own hands. I also won the Eaton award, plus a handsome prize of £10 for the best-kept logbook of the year.

This was a journal filled with technical drawings of the tools we'd made, and its prize-winning quality was more the result of my artistic propensities than my skills as an artisan, which were on the whole unremarkable. The award was presented to me by the workshop manager Ken Wells and the general manager George Hurry, and a photograph taken of the handing over was shown in the *Northern Echo*. In the picture, I am seen smiling gormlessly into the distance wearing my purple velvet embroidered and mirrored jacket, beads and loons, with the managers looking on in what can only be described as embarrassed disappointment.

I looked nothing like the way they would like their engineering protégés to appear, unless it was a psychedelic engineering firm – which it most definitely was not. As it was, they looked like they wished they'd brought their rifles with them. I wasn't the only one who incurred their distaste, though. The second prize of £5 went to another, slightly less flamboyant, but still distinctly unengineer-like fellow called Martin Atkins, who was the drummer in another Yes-style band, and later went on to play with John Lydon's Public Image Limited and his own ensemble, Brian Brain.

I had enjoyed my time at the training centre on the whole and – given the dangerous nature of much of the work that went on there – was glad to have escaped without injury. I did at one point have to go to hospital to have a tiny piece of brass removed from my eye.

This happened when I was filing a brass hinge and a sliver flew up. I was taken to A&E, where my eyeball was painted with some type of blue dye so the metal could be seen and picked out with micro-tweezers, but fortunately by the time I arrived it had worked its way out, and I was in the clear apart from having an itchy eye for a week.

Other boys weren't so lucky. There were numerous cases of 'arc eye', which happened when the flash from an arc weld hit an unprotected eye and sent a searing pain through the head, followed by blindness that could last for weeks.

One unfortunate apprentice sliced his finger off on a guillotine and – worried that he might get into trouble – cleverly flushed the fingertip down the toilet and kept his injured hand behind his back, hoping no one would notice. He couldn't keep this up, of course, and was duly taken to hospital after he was discovered passed out near the dust extractor.

Back at SAB, I spent my weeks moving from department to department – my favourites being maintenance, and upstairs in the drawings office. The maintenance department was taken care of by Mick Metcalfe, who was a big, hairy, bearded ex-Hell's Angel. But behind his brusque exterior was a lovely kind and helpful bloke who looked out for me. The same went for his mate 'Big John', who was a hulking great bloke with the driest of wits. He didn't say much but, when he did say something, it was usually hilarious.

One of my first jobs was to help Big John clear a blockage in the toilet block. I was given a long Dyno-Rod style stick and told to poke it down the toilet whilst John gazed down a manhole. 'You poke that stick down the bog and I'll shout out when the blockage comes by,' he said. So off I went and rammed the bendy pole down the waste pipe. There was silence for what seemed like an age, and I was just about to give up when I heard in the distance the magic words 'Shit's gone by,' and I nearly fell down the pot laughing. He told me it must have been at least three foot long and most likely belonged to Mick, who would probably want it back.

The toilets were a place I grew to know well. Especially on a Thursday morning when the *New Musical Express* came out. I would lock myself in a cubicle and read the paper from cover to cover, which could take well over an hour. One time, some Japanese businessmen were being taken on a tour of the factory and ended up in the washrooms with me trapped in the closet. I thought I had better make a move, but I had been sitting there for an hour with my legs crossed and they had gone dead.

I didn't dare move but I had no choice – they had been in there for quite some time and I had to do something. Unfortunately, when I stood up my legs gave way beneath me and I collapsed onto the cubicle floor laughing with the tingling nerves in my legs. Heaven knows what the management and the Japanese thought on hearing crashing and banging and laughter emerging from behind the door, but thankfully they were ushered out swiftly and I quickly recovered my composure and made a successful exit.

In the course of one of my *NME*-reading toilet sessions, I noticed an article accompanied by a picture of a rather disturbing-looking man, announcing that this grimacing, snarling individual was the future of rock'n'roll. I immediately liked the look of this menacing character, and the write-up sounded right up my street. I had to find out more about this Johnny Rotten and become a fan.

CHAPTER EIGHTEEN

Gavin the Fashionable Bear

'We decided to take the cartoon one step further and make it a reality'

Mum and Dad were still spending the weekends doing the craft fairs. I would go along occasionally, and also joined them every now and again on trips to visit Nanna and Grampy or Grandma and Aunty Ada, but mostly I would stay at home alone.

One weekend, I arranged for my band-mates Wally, John and Geoff and a couple of other people to come over, so that we could drink some beer and play records, which we duly did. And when sufficient beer had been drunk, we began to play a game of truth or dare, or something like it.

To be more precise, it was actually a game of 'let's all make stupid suggestions and do them'. So we all ran around the block in our underpants, and we all hailed a cab and spoke to the driver in backwards-language, and some of us painted our faces blue. All in all it was a remarkable night, and even more so for me, as this was the night that I first had my greens.

My girlfriend Teri had arrived at the party and was soon joining in with the high spirits. It wasn't long before we ended up dallying in my bedroom, and it wasn't long afterwards that we crept beneath the sheets of my bed and grew very fond of each other.

Then, at an inopportune moment, we were disturbed – coitus interruptus, in a compromising situation, whatever you like to call it – as several of my friends leapt upon the bed in a very juvenile fashion, causing an end to the occasion in a way that I had not anticipated. Not the ideal way to lose one's purity, perhaps, but is there ever a right way? Anyway, that's how it happened for me.

The next day, we all met up in town and went to Richmond for a swim, but the first stop was the pub and a couple of pints of Old Peculiar, which is a fine and powerful ale. Following the beers, we went down by the river and lay around in the sun. Nearby was a large man in a pair of swimming shorts, lying fast asleep on the grass. Unfortunately, in his relaxed state, his plums had been set free and were resting on the ground beside him.

Old Peculiar-fuelled bravado led me to take advantage of his disarray by inventing a new game – 'Ball Boules'. We each took a round pebble and took turns at rolling them towards the poor man's jewels, and the nearest one to the 'jack' was the winner. It was bound to happen, and it did. Someone rolled their pebble too forcefully so it hit one of the fellow's cods. He awoke from his slumber, and we all turned and pretended to be deep in conversation, as he looked down to see at least 50 pebbles around his groin area.

Following our game of Ball Boules, we sloped off into the River Swale for a dip, and Teri and I enjoyed ourselves in the privacy of the peaty waters, away from the puerile gaze of last night's pouncing party poopers.

Mum assures me that on her return from that fateful weekend of craft fairs, I took her to one side and grandly proclaimed, 'I am a man now.' While I do not remember saying this, it was certainly a relief to have left behind the ranks of the chaste and entered the adult world at last. And even though my relationship with Teri went the way of so many great romances not too long afterwards, I would always remember her with fondness and gratitude.

*

Trout were by now playing regular gigs at the Bowes wine-cellar, and had begun to establish something of a following. And my bass-playing was proficient enough to enable me to consider myself one of the better bass players in Darlington. The outright best was probably Karl Altdorfer who, with his Red Indian good looks and raw-sounding Rickenbacker, played in the style of Chris Squire from Yes with a band called Imladris.

I knew he surpassed me in terms of conventional musicianly expertise, but I believed that my more maverick approach gave me the edge when it came to star quality. And to hammer home this advantage, I had an eighteen-foot Goodmans speaker fitted into one of my cabinets, giving me the added bonus of being ear-splittingly loud. This meant that my technical deficiencies could be overridden by immense volume – a tactic I had seen Lemmy use very successfully when playing with Hawkwind at the Mayfair Ballroom in Newcastle.

This technique was employed to such good effect at the Bowes one night that the police arrived and turned the sound off. We had exceeded the 90 decibel limit and several of the audience had fled the tiny room with bleeding ears and shattered constitutions. This dramatic turn of events was mainly due to my uncontrollable volume-knob fingers. I was forever nudging up the control, which meant that Trev had to do the same in order to be heard, and Mike would be forced to beat his kit with ever-increasing violence until we sounded like a stadium band wedged into a broom-closet.

Our brush with the law was taken seriously, and I abided by the rules from then on, but I could still wallow in the glory of being the loudest bassist in the region, safe in the knowledge that if anyone tried to beat my record, the Bowes would be closed down.

We began doing gigs outside of Darlington. The first of them was at a pub in Middlesbrough – a modern pub/club set into a shopping centre and devoid of any atmosphere whatsoever. After work I went straight to the haunted rehearsal space and we packed the gear into Trev's brother's van and set off perched on the amps in the back, imagining what the gig would be like.

There would be an audience that had never heard us before who would immediately be transformed into devout Trout fans. Girls would hurl underwear and phone numbers at us, all of them screaming and writhing in undiluted delight, and although Middlesbrough was a mere twenty miles away, it seemed as if we were embarking on a trip to a distant, unconquered land. On arrival, we backed the van up to the rear entrance and unloaded the gear straight onto the stage.

The room in front of us was a cold shell of concrete and plastic with the smell of stale beer permeating every crevice. It was clearly a venue primarily for drinking, with entertainment coming a distant second. Directly in front of the stage was a pool table that we presumed would be removed during our performance. It wasn't. Crouching backstage in our tiny toilet of a dressing room, we knew, as showtime approached and there were only six people in the place, that our predictions of veneration were not to be. And not only that, but the six people in the pub were clearly regulars, and our presence would more than likely be a hindrance to their boozing rather than a pleasant accompaniment.

We considered doing a runner, but were brought up short by the manageress telling us that we had to go on in five minutes and that we should play 'favourites' if we were to get away without any trouble. What she meant by 'favourites' we could only guess at, and so we switched the set list around so the Queen, Bowie and UFO songs were at the forefront and our own compositions were left for the end when we had the six boozers on our side – a strategy that would have no bearing on what actually happened, as we were greeted with cries of, 'Crap!' and, 'Hairy wankers!' the moment we quietly slunk onto the stage and plugged in.

The first two songs went down as expected – to murmurs of discontent and poisonous glowers, accompanied by dark threats to ourselves and our equipment. During the third song, a fight broke out at the pool table right in front of us and the manageress intervened to break it up. This she did with great efficiency and the use of a pool cue that she snapped over the back of one of the bickering players. Throwing that pair of miscreants out automatically reduced our audience by a third.

We struggled on, and after the fourth number Trev tentatively announced that we would be taking a short break – to the muted applause of the remaining four drinkers. As soon as we had sidled off the stage, the manageress pounced on us, revealing that we wouldn't be getting paid due to the lack of response, but if we were to play some Elvis in the second half, she would consider slipping us a couple of quid and promise not to malign us around the town. We had seen her in action with her pool cue and were in no position to refuse her offer to her face.

Instead, we waited until she had gone, backed the van up to the stage, pushed everything into it pronto – wires still attached – and sped away from that hellhole with our illusions shattered, vowing never again to return to Middlesbrough. But our spirits rose with each mile that we drew nearer home, and by the end of the short journey, we'd satisfied ourselves that next week's gig would definitely supply us with all the glory we had predicted and more. Our next booking was at Easington Colliery Working Men's Club. Didn't they sound like they would appreciate a prog-rock power-trio with songs about elves and alfresco dining? Yes, of course they would. And surprisingly, they did.

Easington Colliery is a linear village set in the Durham hinterlands – later to find a strange kind of fame as the location for the film *Billy Elliot*. In those pre-Thatcher days, however, it still harboured a semi-thriving mining population. Perhaps that's why they appreciated us, because spending their working days deep in middle-earth helped them relate to our songs. Or maybe the reason was that having spent so much time in hell they were going to enjoy themselves come what may when they emerged and went for a night out at their local club.

I revisited Easington in the early '90s, after the miners' strike and closure of the pit, and it had become a grey, dejected place, with very little going for it. There was nothing on the street running through the middle apart from two male hairdressers, directly opposite each other as if in battle, and with names that seemed to corroborate the notion of a long-running inter-barber feud. One was called 'Manhair' and the other 'Quiff'.

It seemed that even though time had run out for the town, the unemployed miners could still entertain themselves with grooming competitions. If I were to take sides, I think I would have favoured Quiff, as it seems slightly the more flamboyant of the two. Manhair sounds too much like an ape-shaving establishment for me; the sort of place where rough, tough, hirsute barbarians went to have their foreheads shaved, whereas Quiff may offer a perfumed teddy-boy style, although this is complete conjecture. They may have been fronts for something quite different – opposing families of arms dealers perhaps. Who knows? I wish I did.

Anyway, we did a cracking gig that was much appreciated by the chicken-in-a-basket munching miners, and this time we went home happy – sitting on our amps in the back of the van, praising ourselves to the skies and singing 'Cushy Butterfield' and 'Bonny Bobby Shaftoe' as a thanks to the kind people of the Durham outback.

It was only on reaching home that we realised that we had driven the whole journey back with a cracked axle which could have snapped at any time – hurling us from the road and into some miserable ditch and putting an end to our jollity once and for all. Darkness lurks at every corner whether we are aware of it or not, threatening to put the mockers on buoyant musicians, but not, happily, on this occasion. We had, as a tabloid newspaper might say, 'cheated death', kept aloft by our blithe spirits, post-gig euphoria and the simple fact that the axle didn't snap.

*

Work at SAB ground on. The day would start with Ray's entre-preneurial tales of buying spears from the filming of *Zulu* and selling them on to 'foreign' restaurants, or, alternatively, sexual stories of a deeply unsavoury nature. Apparently there was a man arrested near Ray's house for interfering with horses.

According to Ray, a series of holes dug in the ground had been discovered in fields where horses grazed. These holes were dug by the horse interferer so he could put the unfortunate animal's back legs down them and therefore reach their rear end.

His vile activities only came to light when he thought up a new method which involved an elaborate harness system of ropes hanging from a tree. Unfortunately for the man, he became entwined within the confused mass of his elaborate hoist, and was found dangling in the style of Indiana Jones from the branches of the sycamore tree. Strange fruit indeed.

Ray's response to this disturbing tale was to suggest matter-of-factly that it would have been more sensible for the man to simply take a box with him to stand on.

The first thing I'd do on entering the factory would be put my overalls on, get a cup of tea, and take a trip to the toilet to read the *NME* or the *Sun*. Sitting on the pot in the early mornings, one heard some frightening sounds.

The British workman expelling his previous day's waste can be an earth-moving experience. I have always been very neat and tidy in that department, and taciturn with it, but some of the sounds I heard coming from within those booths were inhuman. Great, deep, guttural growls and grunts would be followed by napalm, muck-spreading, scatter-bomb explosions, forced out of their bodily enclosure by nitroglycerine and plunged into the murky depths like a depth charge.

This traumatic parting of the ways would in turn be followed by curses and oaths directed at the offending waste, as if it were a profoundly unwelcome visitor who had grossly overstayed its welcome. 'Get out, you bastard, and don't come back,' or 'Go on, piss off. You're not welcome, and take your mates with you.' And the men's toilets were just as bad.

I was constantly shifted around the factory in the hope of acquiring a good grounding in the engineering trade, but my favourite place was upstairs in the technical drawing department. Up there, you didn't have to wear a boiler suit, it was clean and tidy and I could draw, which was what I loved doing. Once I had finished drawing what I was supposed to be drawing – a brake-casing or a spring, boss or grommet – I could mess about and play with the drawing equipment for my own ends.

By that time I had given up on my spacecraft pictures and turned to cartoons, and in my spare moments I began producing full-scale strips featuring a character I had invented called 'Gavin the Fashionable Bear'. This animated saga followed the adventures of Gavin – a full-sized Bungle-type bear – in his endless search for stylish garments.

He wandered around naked apart from a trilby hat and a pair of pointed Cuban-heeled boots, looking for outfits that would make him the most fashionable bear in Britain. This meant finding short capes, boob tubes, Y-fronts and false beards – in fact anything that I found funny enough for my bear to be seen in – and his searches led him to places such as wells, magic pantries and aircraft bomb-bays.

I loved to use outmoded speech and words in the text as well

— words like 'Swish', 'With it', 'Clobber' and 'Trendsetter', reclaimed from 1960s pop magazines. Ironic juxtaposition and being deliberately old-fashioned did not feature in comedy then, and these creative devices were a hard sell to my work colleagues, who thought I was mentally disturbed.

But when I took my cartoon strips home to show Geoff, John, Herb and Rob at the Green Dragon, they knew exactly where I was coming from. So we decided to take the cartoon one step further and make it a reality. We decided to become a gang called 'The Fashionable Five'. We would disassociate ourselves from the world and its offerings and dwell in a realm of our own design.

*

Still dressed in my heavily patched jeans and hemp sacking tops draped in beads, I had started making badges. Firstly, they were photos of Hendrix and Roger Dean mushrooms and flying ships, and then I began to make ones with pictures of 'Gavin' and randomly cut-out faces from magazines — people such as TV cowboy Doug McLure and *George and Mildred*'s Yootha Joyce, who were just uncool enough to be cool. My choice of clothing had long been a cause of concern to respectable townsfolk. And my bespoke badge-enhanced appearance, waiting at bus stops on the way home from work, led to me receiving glances from policemen as they passed by in their panda cars.

I presume they had been shown pictures of hippies at Woodstock looking similar to me and imagined that I was delivering a few kilos of Moroccan gold to the outlying areas of Darlington. And so it came to pass that I was eventually arrested and taken to the station for questioning.

Firstly, I was commanded to open my bag and the contents of my Tupperware lunchbox were examined. Once it was determined that what they had suspected as heroin was actually luncheon meat, I was released, after being told to dress more normally and this sort of thing wouldn't have happened in the first place.

I didn't dress more normally and the same thing happened a week later. I was thrust into the back of the panda in front of the bus-stop queue and taken down to the cop-shop where, once again, my lunch was examined.

This time they did a more thorough search and my 'Gavin the Fashionable Bear' cartoons were discovered. The policeman investigating me called in his colleagues to listen as he read out my stories in a mocking tone, completely missing any of the humour and – to my mind – embarrassing himself completely. But to him and his chums I was a deeply retarded hippy who could no more run drugs than tie my shoelace, so I was once again hurled out into the early evening.

When I got home and told Dad, he was spoiling for a run-in with the rozzers himself, and I had to hold him back from going down to the station and having it out with the law. I knew that if he did it would make it more difficult for me, and I had no intention of changing my appearance just to fit in with society and therefore not get arrested. In fact, these experiences had quite the opposite effect. It's simple child psychology: you tell a child not to do something and he or she will do it. And I did it.

I would not be told to conform. It was against every principle I stood for. I didn't want to fit in and be like everyone else; I was an individual and I had my own ideas, and to me then – and in fact

I still believe this – plagiarism is a sin and a crime against people who are capable of original thought. The fact that no copper was going to tell me what to do made me a drop-out. And so I rushed off to Dressers bookshop and bought a copy of *On the Road*, so I could learn about Tuning in, Turning up and Dropping off, pilfer the ideas of Jack Kerouac, and claim them for my own.

*

After reading *On the Road*, I had a bet with the rest of the Fashionable Five that I could hitchhike around Britain in a weekend, and a route was drawn up on the back of a beer mat. My epic journey would take me from Darlington to Cambridge, across to Bristol and back, starting on a Friday night and returning to the Dragon by Sunday.

The following weekend I was ready for the trip. I had spent the week thinking about how Kerouac would have gone about this. I decided that I didn't want to carry a typewriter around with me, nor did I have a bag of amphetamines, bottles of bourbon or any mad arms dealers to visit en route, so the only concession I made was to go downtown in Darlington and buy a jazz hat – a black beret – which I placed at a carefully cocked angle before setting off to hitchhike from Scotch Corner, straight after work on a Friday night.

After standing at the side of the road for approximately twenty minutes, I had thought through the entire trip – sitting in lorry drivers' cabins, listening to their dreary sexual anecdotes gathered from a variety of cheap publications and claimed as their own. Never mind the risk of one of them finding me an appealing substitute, I decided that I had been on the road long enough and I should return to the Dragon and a hero's welcome. I had stories enough to tell — stories of the bus trip to the Scotch Corner roundabout and stories of the bus trip from there to the Dragon. These I could tell all night long over some pints of foaming brown ale, and so that was that.

I did attempt this trip once again a few years later and managed to end up at Grantham with nowhere to sleep. Having buried myself in a bunker on a golf course and got horribly damp, before a further vain attempt to sleep on a field of closely cropped corn, I hastened home, clear in the knowledge that hitchhiking should not be done simply for fun. But that wasn't going to stop me. In fact, I was to become a hitching obsessive.

CHAPTER
NINETEEN

'"And you are a member of the British Army serving with the Green Howards?"'

Another trip we went on was a camping expedition to Ullswater in the Lake District. Myself, Jack and Doc decided – as was now our custom – to hitchhike our way there for a weekend of fun, but we hadn't got far out of town when things started to go sour. Having successfully caught a couple of lifts, we were dropped off at Greta Bridge on the A66 and began walking down the road with thumbs cocked, waiting for another lift. Before too long, a car pulled up and stopped in front of us, but it wasn't the sort of car we required – 'twas a cop car.

The policeman lined us up and asked our names and then commanded us to remain where we were whilst he checked up on us. He proceeded to converse self-importantly with his 'database operative' over the shortwave radio from the front seat of his official vehicle, occasionally gazing back at us with suspicion all over his face. Now and then an eyebrow would be raised; a slow shake of the head and a narrowing of the eyes was accompanied by a downward curved mouth. Eventually he got out of the car and slowly and dramatically walked back over to us.

'OK, you two, clear off,' he said, pointing at Jack and Doc and slinging a hooked thumb over his shoulder.

'Can we wait for our friend?' they enquired.

The response was a barked, 'No, get away from here, I don't want to see your faces again, and your friend here is in a lot of trouble, so I don't think you'll be seeing him for a long time.'

A heavy weight plunged through my body, rather like a house brick being dropped down through my insides, starting out in my brain and landing somewhere around the bottom of my bowels. This strange sensation was rounded off by the small fart that I let go in response to the cop's worrying statement. Jack and Doc left the scene and I was told to get into the passenger seat of the car. The cop got in the driver's seat and stared at me for a while.

'What?' I muttered shakily.

'You know what,' replied the cop.

'What am I supposed to have done?' I expanded anxiously.

Another lengthy silence ensued, and then he took out some notes. 'Are you James Roderick Moir of Hewitson Road, Darlington?'

'Yes.'

'And you are a member of the British Army serving with the Green Howards?'

'No, I am not in the British Army.'

'Yes, you are, and you deserted last week. Your name and description all fit.'

My nerves began to settle the moment I heard this ridiculous accusation. I knew it was all nonsense and so did the cop. He was just wasting a bit of time and he knew it and I knew it.

'I wouldn't be in the army with hair like this, would I?' I

pointed out to him.

'You could have grown it,' he blustered, realising the foolish-ness of this comment even as he uttered the words. The whole tense situation quickly drew to a bathetic close when he got back onto his pretend database, looked at my fingernails and said clearly down the radio. 'No, his fingernails don't fit that descrip-tion.'

He put the radio down, solemnly turned to me and said, 'Seems like you've got away with it, now get out of the car and get away from here as quickly as you can.'

And with that I was ejected and he sped off down the A66. Jack and Doc were waiting a little further up the road, hiding in a ditch, and I took great pleasure in relating to them yet another shocking case of police wasting my time.

We carried on to Ullswater and found a nice campsite right on the water's edge. We did the usual things – drank beer, ate cheese, crept about in the dark repeating things people said around their camp fires, much to their annoyance and our own puerile pleasure – and the following morning we decided to leave *Blue Peter*-style time capsules somewhere.

So we gathered some bits of rubbish pertinent to ourselves and went off to find a photo booth to get our pictures done. Once this mission was accomplished, the photos, the rubbish and a message written in strange runic characters were placed into three baked-bean cans and we set off to find an ideal location for burial.

We climbed hills and dales and eventually found a pine-topped slope overlooking a tarn, and amongst the pine needles we began to dig our holes, each about a foot deep. Having buried our tin cans containing our photos and our cryptic notes, we said a few sacred words of mystery, bowed, and ran off down the hill, hollering and hooting and looking for something else to do.

I have often wondered where that pine-covered hilltop is. We were camping near Pooley Bridge and I don't think we strayed very far. The tins are probably still there and one day I shall return and bury them deeper.

*

That was an average weekend camping trip, and then it was back to work for us all. When I wasn't in the drawing department, I was on the shop floor busy at some task, and one of these tasks was loading and unloading in the bay at the back of the factory.

Lorries would come and go, and the drivers would have a cup of tea whilst their wagon's consignments were being dealt with. I enjoyed doing this: it was good fun operating the forklift. But this apparently simple activity took on a sinister aspect when one of those drivers turned out to have been Peter Sutcliffe, the Yorkshire Ripper.

Around that time there were roadblocks all over the North of England and police were constantly questioning drivers – especially around our area as the Sunderland fraudster had been sending his messages to the police claiming he was the Ripper. I had been in the car with Ray when he was vetted, but Sutcliffe obviously slipped through their net because I had been loading his lorry. We only found out after he had been caught and someone recognised him, checked up on the delivery sheets and there was his name.

This eerie discovery had a grisly postscript. One morning, while the Ripper was still at large, a girl we vaguely knew, who used to drink in the Dragon and was sometimes on our table, had been discovered dead behind a wall on Haughton Road, having been hit over the head with a brick.

This murder was not considered to be the work of the Ripper at the time, as it apparently wasn't his style, but it certainly fitted in with the dates and the location of his visits to the loading bay at SAB. The awful thought that I could have joined him in a cup of tea either before or after he destroyed the life of a friend is quite sickening. It also makes you wonder how many other murderers we might have unknowing contact with in the course of innocently going about our day-to-day business.

Putting aside such macabre speculation in favour of more conventional adolescent remembrances ... I had given my friend Tally some money to buy tickets to see a band at Newcastle City Hall. For some reason I seem to recall that it was Roxy Music, although they weren't a band I would have wanted to see at that time. In any case, it was definitely someone beginning with the letter 'R', because Tally couldn't get tickets for them and so bought tickets for the next band whose name started with that letter. The logic behind this escaped me then, as it does now.

Anyway, he returned with tickets for Ritchie Blackmore's Rainbow – a group I had no desire to see whatsoever, but we had tickets now, so we might as well go. The night of the concert arrived and we decided to pass the half-hour train journey to Newcastle with a bottle of Bell's whisky. I had never drunk whisky before, and would not do so again.

We'd polished off the whole bottle by the time we reached Newcastle, and my head was swimming as we rolled off the train. Tally's suggestion was that we drink ourselves sober. He had heard that this could be done, so we went over the road and into the Yates wine lodge, drank some now mercifully forgotten drink, and wove our way to the City Hall.

Once inside, and feeling extremely nauseous, the lights went up on the stage, the dry ice pumped across it and the first power-chord was struck. At this precise moment, as the crowd lurched forward, I collapsed and was rolled out of a side door by the security, and straight into a dirty Tyneside puddle.

I dragged myself out of the mire, made my way round to the front of the hall and crawled back up the stairs. Reaching the top, I mumbled something drunkenly to the doorman about regaining entrance if he would be so kind, although it didn't sound anything like that. Even though the words, 'Please can I come back inside, I have a ticket and my friend is in there,' were perfectly formed inside my head, my mouth would not respond and what came out was something like, 'Piss come in bacon, a sticket and my fence is there.'

For some unknown reason, the doorman couldn't understand me and I was heave-hoed briskly down the stairs and away into the night. It took me about an hour to find my way back to the station, by which time I had begun to sober up (it's amazing how swiftly alcohol can course through young blood). I caught the train home sick and miserable, vowing never again to touch a drop of whisky, nor to attend a Rainbow concert – a solemn oath which I have upheld, on both counts, to this day.

*

There were two places we used to hang out in town on a Saturday – the Green Tree café, which used to belong to the Golden Egg franchise, and a new/old café which we called the 'In' café. The reason being that this café, which was situated right next door to the Odeon cinema, had been closed down in 1967, and had just reopened with the décor intact, as well as the jukebox having the same selection as it did on closure, making it a new/old café and the 'In' place to be: hence the 'In' café.

It was the décor that drew us to this tiny place: a riot of orange and yellow swirls and walls covered with stuffed animals – squirrels, foxes, owls – all glaring down at us as we dined on hot chocolate and cheese toasties. On the jukebox were tracks by Hendrix, Jefferson Airplane and, a particular favourite of mine, 'House of the Rising Sun' by Frigid Pink – a rowdier version of the old Animals' classic. This became the Fashionable Five's headquarters, and many a plot and plan was hatched here.

One of these schemes was to follow a man we'd seen around the town centre who bore an uncanny resemblance to the actor Terry Scott.

'Have you seen that bloke who looks just like Terry Scott?'

'Yes, shall we find him and then follow him around?'

'Yeah, and why don't we follow him in single file?'

'Good idea, and if he spots us we can all duck into a shop doorway or an alley.'

'And whilst we are hiding in the doorway, we can hum loudly, which might freak him out.'

'Good idea – come on, let's do it.'

So off we went and found the Terry Scott lookalike and followed him about. I don't think he realised for the first few weeks. We quickly became very skilful at ducking away should he turn round, but at some point he must have found out and he snapped, turning and telling us to stop following him. We apologised and gave up our Saturday sport, returning to the 'In' café to concoct a new diversion.

As the Fashionable Five continued to evolve, we celebrated our intensifying exclusivity by honing down our nicknames. John Irvine had already become 'Doccy Deacon', shortened to 'Doc'. Geoff Dent became 'Jiffy Jackson', shortened to 'Jack'. Robert Colebrook was now 'Cot', while Graham Bristow's less than flattering 'Herbert' gradually transformed into 'Herman'. I, for some reason – perhaps because everyone found my name sufficiently compact and/or amusing already – continued to be known as Rod.

*

Having spent our formative years remaining pretty much within the Darlington area, and taking holidays with parents to not too distant pastures, we were all of us getting itchy feet, and plans to explore the more distant reaches of our nation were constantly being batted around. One of these was a hitchhiking/camping trip to Cambridge.

We went in pairs – myself with Jack, and Mike Jackson with someone else. We set off separately and agreed to meet up and find a campsite when we arrived in Cambridge. It seems strange now, in our days of mobile phones and, 'I'll give you a ring when I get there and let you know where I am', but we had no other form of communication, so we decided to be at the main post office on the hour, every hour, until we finally made contact.

Jack and I hitched a ride with a vicar whose car broke down after a few miles. We abandoned him to deal with it on his own, knowing full well that we would shortly be struck down by God for such selfish behaviour. We then, with immense luck – if there was a judgmental deity then he hadn't witnessed our abandonment of the clergyman – got a lift in a National Express coach that was empty and going in our direction. We travelled in style the whole way down and arrived in good time, albeit in a torrential downpour.

As we'd got there first, we decided to make some enquiries as to where the best and nearest place to camp might be. We didn't have to travel far. A man in a Robin Reliant had spotted our rucksacks and pulled over, asking us if we would like a lift to a nearby camp site. He was an old man, of about 70 – wizened and wheezing as he proudly told us that he only had one lung. We shoe-horned ourselves into the tiny car and off we went into the storm.

The camp site turned out to be flooded, and so – the man reckoned – would all the others be, but, no worries, he was a leading light in the university's maths department and since it was the summer holidays and all the students were away, there were plenty of empty rooms that he could let us have. We should go off and meet our friends, have a drink, and come round to his place at 10.30pm and he would sort us out with accommodation.

We all met up at the post office and went off for a drink at a pub called the Fountain, which was tended by the campest man I had ever seen. He was quite a tall and well-built chap, with tight white slacks, a tall blond bouffant hairdo, and long varnished fingernails.

This truly was a new world. A man as camp as that would not be tolerated working behind the bar in a pub in our region. I had never seen such flamboyance and began to sketch him for inclusion in the next episode of 'Gavin'. Some visiting Swedish lads who were sitting nearby had also noticed his theatricality. They leaned over to us, pointing at him and said, in their best English, 'Keep your bottom strong.' This, then, became the catchphrase of the week.

At closing time we made our way over to the old man's house as instructed. We were invited in by a young Chinese boy who was entertaining the old man with some form of t'ai chi whilst he sat in a grubby armchair watching. We were shown our quarters. I had a double bed, Jack had a single behind a curtain, and the other two were given sleeping bags on the floor. We all dropped off but then at about 2am I heard and felt movement in and around my bed. There was a scrabbling, followed by a hoarse whistling sound, and then the movements got closer.

The old man climbed into bed with me. 'Come on,' he said, 'We're all young at heart,' while attempting to slide his hand around my waist.

I froze, petrified and, through a choked throat, said, 'Make one more move and I'll whip you to death with my belt.' I surprised myself with my dramatic statement, but realised that it was probably closer to the truth than I thought. If I were to strike this ancient, one-lunged gnome, he would surely shatter and crumble to dust and I would be held responsible for murder under the most questionable of circumstances.

It turned out that we were, in fact, in his own room and he had selected me as the one to sleep in his bed and therefore subject to his advances. Like any true friend would, I told him that it was

Jack that he should be bothering – although thankfully he didn't – and he proceeded to ask me whether I was a fan of hi-fi equipment. I lay awake all night with my hand on my belt, then woke the others and fled home before dawn. Over the following weeks I was ridiculed consistently as the old man's plaything and when would I be visiting him again? And on and on until the joke finally faded.

*

In April 1977, Doc and Alan Davidson came into the 'In' café raving about a new single they had just bought. It was 'White Riot' by The Clash, and on their recommendation I went off and bought myself a copy, as well as 'Anarchy in the UK' by the Sex Pistols. At last the seed planted by that earlier edition of the *NME* had born glorious fruit. This was to be the turning point.

We had read about the punk rock movement and liked the theories and the style. It fitted in with the way we thought, and the destruction of pompous music seemed to be a good idea, although throughout the entire period of feverishly claiming we thought the prog rock we had adored previously was rubbish, we were all going home and listening to our Van Der Graaf Generator and King Crimson records on the sly. (It was gratifying to discover later that many leading punk rockers were doing exactly the same thing.)

That weekend, everyone went off and cut their hair into the new chopped-up style – apart from me. I agreed with the idea of being unique but (in retrospect, showing still greater loyalty to punk's gospel of individualism) refused to be guided by a doctrine about hair length. So I compromised by cutting myself a ridiculously short fringe whilst leaving the rest long. I looked like an urchin schoolgirl.

There was a real freshness and a liveliness in this new way of thinking. We didn't call ourselves punks, but we certainly went along with the movement's principles, and the oddness of our appearance certainly put us into this class as far as the good townspeople of Darlington were concerned. Amongst these townsfolk were a rival band to Trout with the unsavoury name of Jailbait, who found our personal style deeply loathsome and made this plain whenever we came near them.

On one occasion as we were walking up Posthouse Wynd, there was a cowboy-style stand-off between us and them: us five facing them five, which we found amusing and they found aggravating. 'Poofs,' one of them muttered, sourly, and another added, 'You think you're it, you lot, but you know what, you're not.' This we found even more hilarious, which in turn made them more angry.

Cot, who was entirely unfazed by this dangerous situation and felt the need to pass wind, suddenly exclaimed, 'Ooh dear, I think I'm going to drop one.' Jailbait's drummer, 'Big Fat John', misinterpreted Cot's statement and presumed he was referring to the possibility of attacking one of their number.

'Are you?' he countered, menacingly. 'I bet you don't.' At which point we all cracked up and provocatively rolled about laughing.

It was all too much for Jailbait. We were obviously disturbed and not worth bothering with, and so they left, shaking their heads in despair with comments of, 'You're mental, the lot of you, you should be locked up.' We were looked upon in this way by a lot of people, and we liked it.

*

It was about this time that I realised the moment had come to leave Trout, but we had a gig lined up at Whitby Shipyard and that had to be done. I wanted the music to change to a more punky sound, and so did Mike Jackson, but Trev was adamant that we remain true to our roots and this caused an uneasy atmosphere. There was a final attempt to save the group, and we recruited Wally as a second guitarist, which livened things up a bit, but it still didn't do it for me, and so the gig in Whitby became the last Trout gig ever.

It turned out to be one of the best. Whitby loved us. Perhaps because we knew it was our farewell show (even though nobody in the audience had heard of us) we let rip in a most spectacular style. I tried to speed everything up into a new wave frenzy, and Mike thrashed around furiously wearing his old school uniform. We did two encores and went off back to the promoter's house to celebrate with beer and crisps.

I awoke the next morning in an attic bedroom with a Velux window and a seagull staring down at me. I felt great. Trout were over, and I would form a new band with the Fashionable Five. I took the North Yorkshire Railway trip home through the beautiful countryside, wrote some words that were to become new songs, and then hurled them from the window into the River Esk.

CHAPTER
TWENTY

'Soon we would remove ourselves from our youth and its familiar environs, and implant ourselves in the city of easily accessible red suede shoes'

I n June, Doc and I went to our first punk rock gig – The Stranglers at Middlesbrough Town Hall. Middlesbrough is a bigger town than Darlington as well as having an art college, so it was hardly surprising that there were punks at the concert, and I soon realised that I didn't fit in at all with my patchwork 28-inch flared Levi's. Fortunately, the floor was festooned with safety pins that had fallen from people's outfits. I harvested a number of them, pinned my jeans in tightly into an unfamiliar drainpipe fashion and ripped my T-shirt until I felt punky enough to fit in.

Although The Stranglers didn't really appear to be punks as they all seemed to be ancient – especially Jet Black, the drummer, who must have been nearing 50 even then – they did it for us, and we pogoed our way through the night, finally emerging from the venue thrilled and excited. So much so that we indulged in a spot of graffiti, and after scrawling 'The Clash' on a railway poster at the station we returned home feeling enormously rebellious.

I had decided that I should conform and get my hair cut, and began looking through the *NME* to find a pop star with a style I could copy. Elvis Costello was a geeky young singer whose hairstyle exuded a novel 1950s approach, so I cut out a picture of him and took it into the hairdresser's next to the Stone bridge in Darlington.

The stylist, who favoured the high-topped, bell-shaped 'do', held in shape with bucketloads of hairspray, gazed at the picture for an eternity, wrinkling his nose at it and screwing up his eyes as if he had never seen anything like this in his hairdressing life. This was – by today's standards – a very average haircut and nothing to be confused by, but he grew more and more perplexed, turning the photo upside down and sideways until he felt confident enough to begin.

I emerged from the hairdresser's an hour later looking like a Bee Gee. He had totally ignored the picture and decided to remain true to his own tonsorial instincts by giving me a towering, bouffant, centrally parted 'do' with cylindrical tubes rolling over the ears and round the back. I hurried home, ran straight into the bathroom desperately clutching a pair of scissors and proceeded to attack my hair from every angle, eventually producing an appealing mess that I then dyed with henna, making it a glorious orange. Lovely.

*

With the onset of punk, millions of bands sprang out of nowhere. It was easy to get up on stage now. Musical skills weren't a necessity – it was all about ideas and what you said and looked like – and there were so many new bands to see, I was soon going to two gigs a week.

Siouxsie and the Banshees played at Durham Polytechnic with Sid Vicious on drums. Their set consisted of about fifteen to twenty minutes of 'The Lord's Prayer', and ended with the PA system being turned over into the audience and the hall being evacuated. The whole night lasted approximately half an hour from start to finish, and even within that half hour I was sexually interfered with by a girl who grabbed my hand and forced it onto her breast. Does that qualify as interference? Probably not, especially as I probably squeezed fulsomely, before indignantly withdrawing my mitt and fleeing the scene in tears.

The S.P.O.T.s, or Sex Pistols On Tour (as Johnny Rotten and co. renamed themselves to try and avoid being banned by scandalised local councils across the country) were on at the Kirklevington Country Club. Sadly, I was told at the door that they were a soul group and under no circumstances would I be allowed in looking like I did.

Then there was The Clash at Middlesbrough Town Hall, supported by The Slits, whom I liked very much. And I admired this pugnacious all-woman outfit even more when a young punk who we called 'Hate and War' (on account of him having it painted onto the back of his jacket) was kicked in the neck by Ari Up for attempting to get a look up her skirt.

Another Clash concert I went to found Joe Strummer and his band being supported by the Talking Heads, who were moving music on into areas that I liked, and Richard Hell and the Voidoids, whom I also greatly favoured. It was a classic bill that I had been looking forward to for some time. We got to the Newcastle University venue early, and went to the bar for our tea of nicely heated lager in wonderfully pliant plastic beakers. And then it was time for the bands, but first I needed a wee, so I asked the caretaker where the toilet was.

'On the top floor,' he directed me, curtly. 'Isn't there one any nearer?' I asked.

'No,' he replied. 'But you can go round there if you want,' and he pointed to a dark area under some stairs. Under the stairs I duly went, and soon began to pass lager, but then from out of nowhere a broom hit me round the back of my neck: it was the caretaker.

'You dirty bugger, get out,' he spat, and chased me out of the door with his brush into the cold night air.

I could hear the Voidoids inside the hall from my frozen perch on a bench in the courtyard, and decided that I had been unfairly treated and would regain entry whatever the consequences, so I crept in through a window and back into the gig. Unfortunately, I ripped my trousers on the window latch, and the split grew gradually worse as the night drew on. The inside seam was unravelling, until by the time I left I was wearing what was effectively a maxi skirt and cries of, 'Powdered puff,' pursued me all the way back to the station.

Another time at Newcastle University I had gone to see Generation X. I had little fondness for Billy Idol and his cronies so I spent the evening wandering about. A nice-looking girl was also roaming around. After a while we decided to have a snog and ducked out of the public's gaze and into a storeroom. After 30 seconds we heard a commotion outside, abandoned our spontaneous amour and exited the cupboard, which – unbeknownst to us – had turned out to be the switch room. One of us had inadvertently knocked the stage power switch off and Gen X had been plunged into darkness. We split up and ran in opposite directions, pretending this was not our doing. I never saw her again, but I got quite a power kick from being responsible for the disturbance.

By the time we went to see The Ramones at Newcastle City Hall in December 1977, I had developed a new style of dress which involved me looking like Sid James from the *Carry On* films in a khaki car-coat and trilby hat. This, I thought, conflicted sufficiently with the standard punky gear and leather jackets of The Ramones' fans to allow me to stand out from the crowd, but noticed I was not and so – with a combination of teenage stroppiness and the fact that I thought it would be funny – I sat on a pew chair and looked completely disinterested. So much so that I fell asleep.

This finally had the desired effect. How could anyone snooze through a Ramones concert? And look what he's wearing, the old get. I was, of course, asleep and unaware of the attention until I heard about it later, when it was verified by the rest of the Fashionable Five and also by the fact that someone in the audience had placed a calling card in the brim of my trilby which read 'Twat'.

*

The Fashionable Five had been rehearsing in Doc's bedroom for a few months now and a selection of songs had begun to take shape. They all had a childish sense of naivety about them, which kicked against the pomp and ceremony of the 'Yes' type bands as well as the anger of the punk groups. We wanted to be different to everybody and if possible disliked by all-comers. We would change our name at every gig so we would have no fans and effectively become a non-band.

Amongst the names we chose in pursuit of this objective were 'Bobby and Jackie Charlton's Eerie Mansion', and 'They Called it Rum!' Our songs included 'Cakes and Pop', which was a celebration of teatime treats and 'Fashionable Five' whose banal lyrics were 'Fashionable Five, woah yeah, Fashionable Five, and how! Fashionable Five too right we dance all through the night' sung in German and French and later in Esperanto – the artificial language intended to unite the world which we found hysterically ridiculous.

The evolution of our dogma was codified through a uniform – black slacks, tight yellow jumpers with home-made F.F. badges on the breasts, and a shoe of your choice.

This uniform, combined with our salute – palms of the hands on the temples, with the hands shooting skywards in a 'what have I done now?' kind of way – completed the effect. We were like some demented fascist/communist army whose doctrine was the veneration of infantile nonsense, non-conformity and self-reliance.

By January 1978, we had enough songs to do a gig, and the wheels were put in motion for us to make our historic debut. We were offered a support slot with a young teenage punk group at a school in Darlington. As soon as we turned up at the venue we knew it wouldn't go well, but that didn't bother us, in fact it would be a bonus. We arrived in our uniforms with a drum machine and the Woolworths organ for Cot to play.

Herman had taken over on bass duties as he was the most unproficient bass player anyone had ever heard. He had a great love of reggae music and was under the impression he was a dub master, with his one-stringed bass with numbers glued onto the frets allowing him to count the notes and pluck them with his strangely hooked finger.

Doc and I played guitar in the most rudimentary way and Jack, having no instruments left, took charge of turning the drum machine on and off, and in between, twanged on a Jew's harp.

The kids in the punk band were all about fifteen and their audience were avid fans of the same age, while we were all nineteen and twenty, which put us in the 'old man' category as far as they were concerned. Our music was not at all what they wanted to hear, with our wilful twee-ness, and odes to sweetmeats and astronauts on hang-gliders.

We walked onto the stage and turned the drum machine on. I announced that we were called 'Mike Neville's Mysterious Van' or some such invented-on-the-spot name, and we proceeded to rip through our five songs in the most appallingly slapdash way, much to the disgust of the assembled children.

Unmoved by their undiluted distaste, I proclaimed that we had changed our name to something else similarly confusing – it might have been 'I am the Swaledale Tortoise'. Then we turned the drum machine back on and made a cacophonous row for a further ten minutes, sounding like Can at their riotous peak. And so we left the stage to silence, followed by youthful curses. We packed up our gear and went off to the Dragon to celebrate. Truly this was a momentous victory: we had been successfully reviled.

*

My time at SAB was really beginning to drag, and I had started to think that working as an engineer for the rest of my life might not be such a good idea after all. The money was great and the job security meant that I had no worries on that score.

But the other people who worked there looked like they had no worries either, and they also looked like they were slipping into a kind of boredom-induced madness – a production-line-generated fixation on the mundane. Conversations revolved around Page Three stunners, tyre remoulds and ways of escaping the life they led by disappearing to Spain and an English pub.

I never understood that type of holiday where you go to some dismal resort on the near Continent and install yourself in an inferior version of the kind of place you go to every week at home to drink away the days. Lots of men at the factory went on such trips and I suggested they might save their money and sit in their local pub for a fortnight, but this idea was laughed at on the grounds that Spain was hot and sunny – although to me the fact that they were planning to spend all their time inside a boozer made this argument redundant.

I didn't want to end up like that, so I decided to leave. By the end of the year, I would have fled. Never mind the consequences: this was just the way it had to be.

*

Herman had bought a car. We all chipped in, and for £50 he got a Morris Traveller, which is a Morris Minor turned into a station-wagon with the American-style 'Woody' rear end. The back of this distinctive vehicle was encased in a pine framework, giving it the appearance of a mobile greenhouse – an effect enhanced by the fact that it had mushrooms growing from out of the wood.

It was a fabulous car, though: it was our Fashionable Five staff car, and it fitted in with our look entirely. Even Herman's driving skills, which were tremendously erratic due to him being both scatterbrained and partially sighted (although he wasn't aware of this at the time), suited our calculatedly haphazard overall style.

We decided to drive the staff car down to the Norfolk Broads where we had booked a holiday on a river cruiser, and away we went – weaving merrily down the A1 until we ran out of oil and the car ground to a smoky halt at the side of the road. None of us was a proper driver. We weren't to know that a car had to have oil in it to make it go – we thought petrol would be enough, but no, we were wrong, so off we went to get some oil. This being done, we continued on to Beccles in Norfolk where we were to pick up the boat, hired from Blake's, at the boatyard.

This was great. We were in command of a river craft, and we hammered it hard, travelling as far as we could each day, mooring at night outside a waterside tavern and spending our evenings in the company of beer. I was in heaven. It was so beautiful – just like that Children's Film Foundation movie I had seen at the ABC film club all those years ago. There were sandwich terns and reed warblers and cows grazing in Constable fields and life was good. Hoorah for the Norfolk Broads and its tranquillity.

Then the harmony was disrupted as we sailed into Norwich and moored up for a weekend on the town. We went to see Johnny Moped at some little dive and it was one of the funniest gigs I've ever been to. Firstly he insulted the audience by calling them a bunch of Guinness-swilling farmers. Then the guitarist,

Slimey Toad, climbed up the PA stack with his guitar and got himself wedged between the speakers and the ceiling so he had to be prised out by the rest of the band. Once out, he requested the announcement of the winning raffle-ticket numbers as he was worried that they had been read out whilst he was in his former predicament. This further infuriated Johnny Moped and the tension on the stage was electric.

The following night we went to see the Nipple Erectors, who featured Shane McGowan on vocals. A gawkier man I had never seen and we celebrated this by inventing some new dances. We already had a few unique ones in our repertoire – 'The Mantis', which was simply a representation of the movements of the sinister insect predator; 'The Sharp', an angular robotic gyration; and 'The Dying Fly', where we would do freeform movements finishing with us all collapsing into a heap at the end of the song. But it was on this night that we developed our two most dynamic dances.

'The Death Run' involved us taking turns at running head-long into a wall at full speed and smashing into it regardless of injury. This was a great success, until we were cautioned by the security and had to abandon it, so another routine was concocted, 'The Relay'.

This worked exactly as you would expect. One of us would run around the perimeter of the hall and touch the next runner, who would do the same throughout the duration of the song. This was too much for the organisers of the concert and we were asked to leave and/or grow up. We apologised and agreed to the former (though we could make no promises with regard to the second part of the bargain).

After returning the boat to the yard, we decided to continue on to London. So off we went again in the Morris Traveller. Herman's negotiation of the capital's intimidating road network was frightening in the extreme, but we managed to get to where we wanted without physical scars and booked into a hotel in Sussex Gardens near the Marylebone Road.

We had great expectations of London nightlife, but we didn't really know where to go and ended up at some bar in Mayfair that was populated solely by rich Arabs and prostitutes. When we asked at the bar for directions to the 100 Club and the Vortex and other places we had read about where we might be able to display our dance routines, we were greeted with slowly shaken heads and the suggestion that we return to our hotel pronto for our own safety. And having no better alternative, that's exactly what we did.

The next day, after gently removing an old woman who had decided to sleep on the bonnet of our staff car, we went off to see the sights. The sight we really wanted to see was the Kings Road. It was just what I had expected – a peacock display of clothes and hairstyles. We threw ourselves into the shops and bought as much new-wave finery as we could afford, my favourite purchase being a pair of red suede Cuban-heeled Chelsea boots, just like the ones I had drawn on Gavin the Fashionable Bear. I couldn't stop talking about them and showing them to passers-by.

We continued on to Vivienne Westwood's Seditio-naries and peered in through the window, like urchins outside a Victorian cake shop, or rather yokels who were too scared to enter. And so we ran off to the pictures in Leicester Square to see *Alien* instead.

At that time it seemed pretty much the entire nation was on strike, and Leicester Square was a mountain of black bin bags –

piled 30 feet high, stinking and covered with rats. In fact, most of London was a sea of rubbish sacks, but the image of that particular mountain of waste – that monumental heap of detritus, sweepings and dross, crawling with vermin and maggots – has remained with me to this day.

It was time to return to the North, but that trip to London consolidated ideas of moving, en masse, to try our luck in the place The Clash and the Sex Pistols had come from. Soon we would remove ourselves from our youth and its familiar environs and implant ourselves in the city of easily accessible red suede shoes.

I told Mum and Dad of my intentions to leave home and follow in Dick Whittington's footsteps. I think this news was probably not unexpected, and might even have come as something of a relief. But what would I do for a job?

Herman, who was working in the Civil Service, had already got a transfer to London, and we all decided to follow suit. I arranged an interview for a position in the Social Work Service – not a job I planned on keeping, but a way of getting down there and paying my way. So I took another trip down to London and booked myself into the same hotel in Sussex Gardens that we stayed in before. Only this time I was alone.

It was grey and miserable and I was given a room in the attic. I lay on the tiny bed in the strangely silent dimness and wondered if I had made a mistake, but I knew it was time for me to leave home.

I batted the melancholia away, slipped on my red suede boots and went out to see what was happening at the Marquee in Wardour Street (I had done some research this time). It turned out to be Joe Jackson, of whom I wasn't such a great fan, but I could still make an impression with my footwear. So in I went, and had me a real good time.

The interview was a success and I was offered a position as a clerical officer in the SWS at Tottenham Court Road starting in January. And Herman had secured us a flat in Arodene Road in Brixton, ready to move in.

*

Christmas was a lively but contemplative time back in Darlington. Before long I would be gone and – inevitably – that time came sooner than expected. On a freezing morning in January 1979, Jack and his dad turned up at Hewitson Road. There was a blizzard blowing and I loaded up my few paltry belongings into the van in about five minutes.

Mum had tears welling in her eyes as I left and Dad had one of those 'You can do it' looks on his face – a benign expression of fatherly reassurance. Lois, too, was beginning to fill up, and I was no good at goodbyes. So with a carefree 'See yer' – as if I was off to the pub on a Friday night – I got into the van, and we slowly trundled off into the raging blizzard, the unknown, the blank page.